# Buy Me!

'An excellent read for anyone wanting to improve their ability to persuade others. *Buy Me!* covers all of the key areas needed to be a more effective communicator and salesperson.'

**Neal Gandhi, Author of *Born Global*, Entrepreneur and Investor**

'… An incredibly useful, pragmatic and practical guide that should be read by all those searching for a framework for building a successful career and, perhaps, a successful journey through life. At whatever stage you are at in your career or life, this book contains information that will enable you to improve "You" – if that's what you want to do! An enjoyable and easy read.'

**Roger Skinner, former Strategy & Business Development Director with Ally Financial Services Inc. and The Lombard Group.**

'A truly inspiring read that is a must for anyone in business with aspirations to stand out from the crowd.'

**Julian Humphreys, Managing Director, P2 Performance Squared Ltd**

# Buy Me!

## Ten Steps
## to Selling Yourself
## in Business

Adam Riccoboni
and Daniel Callaghan

MICHAEL O'MARA BOOKS LIMITED

First published in Great Britain in 2011 by
Michael O'Mara Books Limited
9 Lion Yard
Tremadoc Road
London SW4 7NQ

A CIP catalogue record for this book is available from the British Library.

Papers used by Michael O'Mara Books Limited are natural, recyclable products made from wood grown in sustainable forests. The manufacturing processes conform to the environmental regulations of the country of origin.

ISBN: 978-1-84317-654-1

1 2 3 4 5 6 7 8 9 10
www.mombooks.com

Cover design by ab3design
Designed and typeset by ab3design
Printed and bound in Great Britain by Clays Ltd, St Ives plc

This book is dedicated to our parents,
who gave us everything:
Paul & Elaine, Gerry & Carol

# Contents

# Acknowledgements

We would like to thank and acknowledge 3H Partners for their invaluable help and direct contributions to writing this book, including:

- Dr Davide Sola, Associate Professor of Strategy, ESCP Europe

- Dr Jérôme Couturier, Associate Professor of Strategy, ESCP Europe

- Cristina Raicu, for contributions to Step 5: Empathy

- Alisa Gusakova, for contributions to Step 9: Managing the Media

- Francesco Maselli, for contributions to Step 10: Leadership

- Sandro Cuzzolin, for contributions to Step 7: Going the Extra Mile

- Saurav Majumder, for contributions to Step 3: Personal Presentation

- Alexandre Vigneron, for contributions to Step 6: Under-Promise and Over-Deliver

We would also like to thank our team at MBA & Company including Romy Fawehinmi.

# Introduction

'If we all did the things we are capable of doing, we would literally astound ourselves.'
**Thomas A. Edison**

There is a broad choice of business and self-development books on the bookshop shelves. These books can 'help you win friends and influence people', achieve 'confidence', be a 'brilliant manager' and show you 'how to get rich'. It is now even possible to read books purporting to provide a '30-Day MBA', a '10-Day MBA' and – for the really time-strapped – an '80-Minute MBA'. This is even more startling knowing that many reputable business schools would charge in excess of $100,000 in fees and require attendance of a one- or two-year full-time course before awarding an MBA.

So, why have we had the audacity to write *Buy Me! Ten Steps to Selling Yourself in Business*? The simple answer is that learning how to 'sell yourself' is the most important skill you can have in your working life. Selling yourself is crucial to influencing people, to having confidence, to being a brilliant manager and to becoming rich. (It won't, however, give you an MBA!)

## Selling yourself is the key to success

The impact you have on your life will be fundamentally determined by how well you sell yourself. Selling yourself is the single most important skill you could have in your career. It is vital to every aspect of commerciality, and convincing others to 'buy you' is the secret to unlocking your full potential.

Ask yourself:

- Do people recognize your full potential when they meet you?
- Are all your qualities truly utilized at work?
- Are you having the impact on your life that you aspire to?

## Selling yourself is essential in the corporate world

Consider all the times you need to promote yourself directly in your working life: writing a CV, attending a job interview, convincing your colleagues of a new idea, attaining more responsibility from your boss, gaining a promotion, receiving a pay rise, etc. However, selling yourself is also necessary in all aspects of business, as people do not just buy your company, products or services, they buy you. It is vital in winning a new client, managing teams, public relations, establishing a strategic partnership, to name just a few examples.

## Selling yourself is crucial as an entrepreneur

To be an entrepreneur it is essential that you have the ability to sell yourself to others. Initially, you have to sell a concept to the world, with the only physical representation of the business being you. When seeking funding for your venture, selling yourself is absolutely key – venture capitalists or angel investors do not just assess your great business idea, they also assess you.

# People at the top sell themselves all the time

Business leaders or CEOs are generally experts at selling themselves. Their role is to profitably grow a business and how they sell their own values, vision and strategy is vital to that success. Likewise, political leaders do not only present policy programmes; they also need to 'sell' themselves so that you choose to 'buy' them through voting for them.

The modern politician also sells his/her nation on the international stage. For example, in 2010 British Prime Minister David Cameron led a sales expedition of forty-three British business leaders to China. Cameron pledged to sign forty trade deals – but he was outdone by French leader Nicolas Sarkozy who had secured 12.48 billion Euros of French goods to China shortly before. Many celebrities now 'sell themselves' so effectively that they have become a 'brand'; for every big company like Apple or McDonalds, think of JLO (Jennifer Lopez), David Beckham or Madonna.

# The world is shaped by people selling themselves

The economy is a marketplace in which goods and services are transferred. However, there is not an objective criterion for what makes a good product or an excellent service. Everything in the business world is entirely subjective – that is, its value is based completely on what other people think. The most flourishing people in business have convinced others that they themselves, or the products and services they can provide, are highly valuable.

These people are not necessarily any more intelligent or any more capable than anyone else. In fact, many successful people have a number of flaws and weaknesses. For example, the celebrated entrepreneur Richard Branson failed to achieve any academic qualifications at school and was arrested by the police, before setting up a lucrative corporation. However, these people – and Richard Branson especially – are highly skilled at selling themselves.

## Selling yourself is now more important than ever

In the modern world it is paramount that you know how to promote yourself no matter what job you have. The 'job for life' model of the 1950s, in which you could stay in one company for most of your career, has ended. It is now just as important to be 'employable' as it is to be employed. You will need to sell yourself into a number of different jobs, and then into a number of different businesses. The people you deal with will not just buy from you out of convention. They will be spread across the globe, and will have their own approach to business. New businesses are emerging – and old businesses failing – every day. Even giant investment banks such as Lehman Brothers, or entrenched high-street shops such as Woolworths, can disappear overnight. In the digital age, business models are changing more quickly than ever before.

## We know this works

As business professionals, we know the importance of selling yourself from our own careers. We have studied and worked at some of the best business schools in the world such as ESCP Europe, ranked number one in the world for Master in Management by the *Financial Times*, and

IESE, ranked number one in Europe and number five in the world for MBA by *The Economist*. We have raised hundreds of thousands of pounds in investment from venture capitalists. We have sold to leading organizations in the private, public and voluntary sectors. We have established our own company, MBA & Company, and been featured in *The Economist*, *Business Week* and the *Financial Times*. Our company is based on an understanding of how people can sell themselves, as we enable highly skilled MBA holders to sell themselves directly to leading companies for different projects. We believe that in the future individuals may not be tied to one company, but will instead sell their skills and knowledge for the highest price through new media platforms.

So how do you sell yourself? Should you blow your own trumpet to everyone who will listen? Boast at every opportunity? Mass email a list of your qualities to all your contacts? Rent a billboard and poster your face across the City? Perhaps not ...

## This book will help you do it

This book will give you the tools you need to sell yourself and achieve success in your life. It will show you exactly how truly accomplished people – from Julius Caesar to Warren Buffett – have achieved success. It will provide you with the latest management knowledge from leading academics and universities. It will teach you a simple step-by-step process to sell yourself successfully every time. Follow the steps presented on the book and you will:

- Gain more confidence
- Learn how to recover more swiftly from challenging setbacks

- Take control by letting go of your anxieties
- Network effectively for business and pleasure
- Converse on topics you previously felt were beyond your reach
- Move outside your comfort zone and thrive in previously 'no-go' areas
- Form good, impactful connections with others
- Discover how to enjoy your job and find satisfaction in the workplace.

# Step 1:
# Self-belief and Confidence

'Confidence can get you where you want to go, and getting there is a daily process. It's so much easier when you feel good about yourself, your abilities and talents.'
**Donald Trump**

## Why do you need self-belief and confidence?

The first step in selling yourself is developing self-belief and confidence. For someone else to believe in you, you must first believe in yourself.

As former US President Lyndon B. Johnson put it, 'You've got to believe in what you are selling. What convinces is conviction. You simply have to believe in the argument you are advancing; if you don't, you're as good as dead. The other person will sense that something isn't there.'

# How this chapter will help you develop self-belief and confidence

*Learn how to develop your self-belief and confidence, including:*

*Finding your self-belief:*
- *Set your target*
- *Understand your qualities*
- *Think through your business values*
- *Define your Unique Selling Points (USP)*

*Displaying confidence:*
- *Project positive body language*
- *Make eye contact*
- *Smile warmly*
- *Stay calm under pressure*
- *A virtuous cycle*

## Finding your self-belief

There can be no substitute for genuine self-belief and there is nothing more compelling than confidence. Yet it is a myth that most people are confident. The majority of people would like to feel more sure of themselves. Generally, people feel self-assured in some situations and not in others. For example, people who are confident at making a business presentation may be shy at a party; people who are confident when asking someone on a date may be nervous at a job interview.

Also, confidence is not something you are born with or without. You can nurture and develop it through the right mindset.

The following exercises will help you develop self-belief and confidence by identifying your target, your qualities, your business values and by revealing your Unique Selling Points (USPs).

## Set your target

In order to achieve success, you need to know where you want to go in your life. Your target is your ambition or aspiration, how you want your life to be. Your target is also related to your values. For example, if you are someone who believes in generosity and charity, perhaps working in the voluntary sector would be right for you. If you are someone who believes in competition and challenge, perhaps working in investment banking would be right for you.

1. Close your eyes and imagine that your career has gone very well. Picture yourself in ten years' time. You are truly successful and happy. See yourself.

2. People are telling stories about what you have achieved; think about what it is they are saying that makes you feel happy.

3. Why are you happy? Is it from wealth? Is it from security? Is it from fame? Is it from helping others?

4. Think about what you have achieved and let this help you understand what you want to attain in the future.

This is your target and what this book will help you achieve.

## Understand your qualities

You have unique strengths that only you possess: your qualities.

Take a pen and paper.

1. Think back to when you were sixteen years old.

2. Write down what you did that year (who you were living with, where you went, who you spent time with).

3. List your achievements for that year. Write down each success.

4. Go back and answer steps 2 and 3 for each year until the present day.

5. Take the year with the most achievements and write down what personal qualities enabled you to achieve these things.

6. These are your qualities; write down at least five of them here:

Your qualities

Quality 1: _____

Quality 2: _____

Quality 3: _____

Quality 4: _____

Quality 5: _____

## Think through your business values

Now you know where you are going and realize why you can achieve it, you need some rules: these are your values. These show what you consider important in life and shape your behaviour. Look at the table below and underline all the values that appeal to you the most.

Acceptance  Accomplishment  Acknowledgement  Adoration
Adventure  Ambition  Being the best  Belonging  Bravery
Brilliance  Certainty  Challenge  Charity  Confidence  Conformity
Conviction  Cooperation  Correctness  Creativity  Credibility
Decisiveness  Diversity  Education  Empathy  Enjoyment
Entertainment  Excellence  Expertise  Fairness  Faith  Fidelity
Firmness  Flexibility  Friendliness  Fun  Generosity  Growth
Happiness  Harmony  Honesty  Humour  Imagination  Impact
Impartiality  Independence  Ingenuity  Inspiration  Integrity
Intelligence  Inventiveness  Justice  Kindness  Knowledge
Leadership  Love  Loyalty  Making a difference  Optimism
Originality  Outrageousness  Passion  Peace  Perceptiveness
Perfection  Perseverance  Persuasiveness  Philanthropy  Popularity
Power  Precision  Preparedness  Professionalism  Realism
Reason  Reasonableness  Recognition  Relaxation  Reliability
Religiousness  Resourcefulness  Respect  Self-control  Selflessness
Self-reliance  Sensitivity  Sharing  Simplicity  Sincerity
Skilfulness  Speed  Spirituality  Spontaneity  Strength  Success
Support  Supremacy  Sympathy  Teamwork  Thoroughness
Thoughtfulness  Tidiness  Timeliness  Traditionalism
Trustworthiness  Truth  Understanding  Unflappability
Uniqueness  Unity  Usefulness  Utility  Virtue  Vision  Warmth
Wealth  Wilfulness  Willingness  Wittiness  Wonder

Of the values you have underlined, write down the five that appeal to you the most here:

Your business values

Value 1: _____

Value 2: _____

Value 3: _____

Value 4: _____

Value 5: _____

## Define your Unique Selling Points (USPs)

Combining your qualities and values can uncover your Unique Selling Points (USPs). These are skills that you possess in business and show how you will achieve your target.

To define your USPs, think of your main achievements in education and your experience in the workplace.

Now relate each of your key features/qualities and values to these USPs. For example:

- I achieved A grades at school because of my strength of *dedication* and my value of *education*.

- I implemented a new system at work because of my strength of being *organized* and my value of *creativity*.

1. _____

_____

2. _____

_____

3. _____

_____

4. _____

_____

5. _____

_____

Change each sentence to generic instead of specific. For example:

- I achieve at education because of my commitment to learning.

- I implement new systems at work because of my strength at being organized.

Write each sentence below as these are your USPs.

Your unique selling points

1. _____

_____

2. _____

_____

3. _____

_____

4. _____

_____

5. _____

_____

You can be proud of your USPs – only you have them and they are based on your real experience, strengths and values. In Step 3: Personal

Presentation (see pages 55-68), we will also show you how to present these on your CV and in Step 9: Managing the Media (see pages 141-59) we will look at how you can present them on websites such as Linkedin.com.

# Displaying confidence

> ❝ Honestly speaking, what kind of people get to become rich? Whatever qualities the rich may have, they can be acquired by anyone with the tenacity to become rich. The key, I think, is confidence. Confidence and an unshakeable belief that it can be done, and that you are the one to do it. ❞
>
> **(Felix Dennis, *How to Get Rich*, 2006)**

Self-belief is vital to your success, but appearing over-confident and egotistical can be counterproductive. Boasting about achievements and deliberately making yourself the centre of attention can be perceived as arrogance. Project your self-belief and confidence by being positively engaged with other people.

## Project positive body language

Research has shown that 90 per cent of all human communication is based on non-verbal cues. You therefore need to be careful with the body language you project and avoid the negative associations of particular body language cues. For example, hanging your head low projects a lack of self-confidence; folding your arms across your chest can be seen as a defensive or an uninterested stance; slouching in a chair suggests you're unprepared or that, deep down, you feel you're not up to the task at hand.

## Make eye contact

There are few aspects of non-verbal communication more important than eye contact. The eyes are known as 'the windows to the soul', transmitting your emotions and intentions to others. In the corporate world, making good eye contact is the first test you face at every meeting.

Ensure you look directly into the eyes of the person you are speaking to. If there is a group of people, make an effort to look into the eyes of each person equally. Even when just listening to someone, look into their eyes and concentrate fully on what they are saying. Positive eye contact projects confidence, transparency and sincerity.

## Smile warmly

Smiling is so simple and yet such an immensely powerful way to build rapport with people. Professor James V. McConnell, a biologist and animal psychologist at the University of Michigan, found through research that people who smile more are better at managing, teaching and selling. Smiling is so effective that many sales organizations encourage their sales people to smile while speaking on the telephone, even though no one can actually see them. Smiling is also contagious and will encourage others to smile, feel more positive and, as a result, be more open to your ideas and proposals.

## Stay calm under pressure

Many working situations involve stress and pressure. In such situations it is necessary to maintain a positive attitude, especially if there are clients or colleagues present who may perceive your anxiety as a sign of inefficiency. Staying calm under pressure also forms the basis of good management, as effective leadership involves being solution-orientated and level-headed in difficult circumstances.

## A virtuous cycle

Dr Rob Yeung, a psychologist and coach, explains in his book *Confidence: The Art of Getting Whatever You Want* that there is a 'virtuous' cycle between behaving confidently and feeling confident:

> Psychologists call it the principle of retrospective rationality. Your brain likes to believe that you're behaving in a fashion that is consistent with your beliefs. So if you start behaving as a confident person, your brain tries to explain your behaviour by forcing your mind to believe you are a confident person.

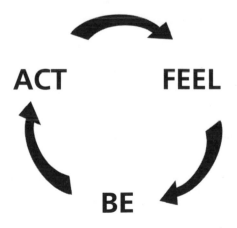

ACT    FEEL

BE

## Case study:
## Donald Trump, self-belief and confidence

Donald Trump's career wonderfully illustrates how self-belief and confidence are crucial to selling yourself and succeeding. After graduating from the Wharton School of the University of Pennsylvania, Trump joined his father's business, building apartment complexes in Queens and Brooklyn. However, Trump gravitated towards Manhattan, the most glamorous and wealthy part of New York. He wasn't fully content having a stable job and a good living; he wanted to accomplish something great and make a powerful statement.

> I like thinking big. I always have. To me it's very simple; if you're going to be thinking anyway, you might as well think big. Most people think small, because most people are afraid of success, afraid of making decisions, afraid of winning. And that gives me a great advantage. (Donald Trump with Tony Schwartz, *The Art of the Deal*, 1987)

### Think big ...

Trump moved to a small apartment in Manhattan and scanned the area for property development opportunities. He found a disused waterfront site in a rundown area that was notorious for high crime levels. At the time, New York was going through a difficult period – it had defaulted on bonds it had issued, causing a financial crisis as a result. Property prices were falling. There were even rumours that the City would go bankrupt.

Trump managed to arrange a meeting with the company that owned the waterfront site, Penn Central. Although only twenty-seven years of age, Trump impressed the executive responsible not only with the proposal but also as a person. With no money down as a deposit, Trump was granted the rights to purchase two waterfront sites from Penn Central at a cost of $62 million.

He then had to find a way of developing the site, and seized on the idea of having a state convention centre that was being developed relocated there. Channelling his self-belief into promotion, Trump waged a campaign in the media, highlighting the benefits of having a convention centre on his waterfront site, and emphasizing the disadvantages of using the other areas under consideration. He targeted key politicians, arguing the case for the overall benefits this kind of regeneration would have on New York City. He won the deal, and the convention centre moved to his site, netting him over $800,000 in fees.

## ...Think bigger ...

For Trump's next deal, he aimed bigger. Penn Central offered him rights to a huge hotel, the Commodore, which had become dilapidated and was losing money. Still only twenty-seven, he was trying to buy and develop a 1,500,000-square-foot building into a 1,400-room hotel. Trump had a three-pronged strategy:

- get professional management for the hotel

- receive tax abatement from the City

- find financing from an investor.

For professional management, he went straight to the top of a large hotel chain, the Hyatt, where he convinced the owner, Jay Pritzker, to strike a deal in which the Trump Organization developed the site and Hyatt managed it. For tax support – after a long campaign, again leveraging coverage in the media – Trump won a forty-year tax abatement from the City worth tens of millions of dollars. On financing, after being turned down by many banks, he won investment from two institutions: Equitable Life Assurance Society for $35 million and Bowery Savings Bank for $45 million. Trump added an eye-catching design, using reflective glass for the outside of the hotel and brown Paradiso marble for the interior lobby. The renamed and relaunched Grand Hyatt Hotel was soon making operating profits of $30 million a year.

## Build towers

Shortly afterwards, Trump put together an even bigger deal, which saw the construction of Trump Tower – the tallest residential building in New York. Over the following years, he grew from strength to strength and expanded into the gaming business, buying some of the most prominent casinos in Atlantic City. He did fall into severe financial problems in the 1990s but bounced back in 2001 when he built the Trump World Tower in Manhattan.

Today, Donald Trump owns several million square feet of prime Manhattan real estate. He is also a media celebrity, famed recently for taking part in the US version of *The Apprentice* (the television show in which hopeful young business people vie for the chance to work for his organization). His name has become synonymous with the ambition and the success of New York City itself.

There are few better examples of the power of self-belief and confidence than a New York City skyscraper with your name on it.

# ✓ What you have learned about self-belief and confidence

In this chapter, you have developed your self-belief and confidence by identifying your qualities, values, targets and USPs. This chapter has highlighted what you want, what you aspire to and how you will achieve it. You have also learned how to project confidence the right way by interacting with other people in a positive and engaged manner. You have consequently achieved the first step to selling yourself successfully: Self-belief and Confidence.

# Step 2:
# Personal Preparation

'You only have to do a very few things right in
your life, so long as you don't
do too many things wrong.'
**Warren Buffett**

## Why is personal preparation useful?

Preparation is crucial to success in business. As the American car racer
Bobby Unser put it, 'Success is where preparation and opportunity
meet'. There is nothing more damaging to your credibility than being
unprepared. Conversely, being prepared has many benefits, including
enhancing your understanding and enabling you to be more effective,
making you appear more professional and increasing the trust that
other people have in you.

# How this chapter will help you with personal preparation

*Learn how to prepare for business, including:*

*Pre-sales preparation:*

- *Analyse your market*
- *Conduct company research*
- *Rehearse your pitch*
- *Use references*
- *Create your value proposition*
- *Write an elevator pitch*

*Sales preparation:*

- *Build rapport*
- *Go for the top*
- *Leverage your network*
- *Get data*
- *Structure a sales call*
- *Structuring an email*
- *Pre-meeting preparation*
- *Follow up*
- *Achieve high volume*
- *Client Relationship Management (CRM)*

# Pre-sales preparation

The importance of preparation is a lesson we learned the hard way. Shortly after we started working, we were invited to a business meeting with the HR Director of a FTSE 50 company. We presented the excellently qualified team available to complete the project for the client. However, we didn't have answers for all the questions the client had sent to us previously by email. Also, our presentation was missing some pages. However, the meeting seemed to go brilliantly; the HR Director laughed and joked with us and told us he would be in touch soon. We waited expectantly for a positive on the deal.

However, a week later, we received an email informing us that we hadn't got it. Surprised to lose a deal we were counting on, we telephoned the client immediately to clarify why they had decided not to work with us. They explained they didn't like the way we had presented with some pages missing and they were also not impressed

> ❛ When I started out in business, I spent a great deal of time researching every detail that might be pertinent to the deal I was interested in making. I still do the same today. People often comment on how quickly I operate, but the reason I can move quickly is that I've done the background work first, which no one usually sees. I prepare myself thoroughly, and then when it is time to move ahead, I am ready to sprint. ❜
>
> **(Donald Trump, *Trump University Real Estate 101*, 2006)**

that we didn't have answers for the questions they had sent in advance of the meeting. The client bluntly explained that it wasn't the proposition that they didn't buy, it was us.

As painful as this was to hear initially, it was actually the best feedback we could have received. It clearly highlighted the need to prepare in advance of doing business. Since then, preparing thoroughly has greatly improved our careers and, subsequently, our lives.

## Analyse your market

The first thing you should prepare for is an understanding of the market you want to sell to. This will enable you to understand which companies are your ideal clients and which executives within the organization you need to talk to.

Your research should include:

- **The overall industry** – is the market growing or shrinking, what are the main challenges for companies?

- **The primary players** – who are the key companies and institutions?

- **Which sector is most suited to your services?** – which companies need your services the most (banking, legal, engineering, etc.)?

- **What executives are the most appropriate for you to target?** – HR Directors, Marketing Directors?

In order to complete an effective market analysis, you can follow three phases:

1. **Desk-based research** – Use the Internet and read books, magazines, etc. to understand everything about a particular topic. This will enable you to come up with certain ideas known as 'hypotheses'.

2. **Validation of findings through interviews** – Test the ideas you developed from your desk research by interviewing real people and asking them their views on your hypotheses.

3. **Conclusions and recommendations** – Update the desk research in phase 1 with the extra information from the interviews in phase 2, fine-tune your ideas and make conclusions.

Now you also understand the overall market, which will make you much more useful and convincing to your clients.

## HINT BOX

*How do you conduct research interviews?*

*Interviews should always be aimed at getting the information you need today, and building a relationship for tomorrow. Prepare in advance by thinking about what questions the person can answer usefully. Introduce yourself, introduce the interview and introduce the topic. When asking questions, use the process: Question, Listen Attentively and then Summarize. At the end, sum up the key points, ask if there is anything else the interviewee would like to add, and then finally make a detailed record of the interview.*

## Conduct company research

Before approaching suitable executives – either by telephone, email or in person – research the company online, paying particular attention to:

- **Their company website** – company history, branding, mission, values

- **Services** – the business the company performs and what makes it unique

- **Annual accounts** – if these are available, they are particularly helpful in providing information on the company strategy and plans

- **Competitors** – this will be one of the key areas of concern for your client companies, influencing their strategy and positioning in the market

- **Executives** – attempt to research the executives themselves. Using an Internet search engine can often provide information on the executives – through Linkedin profiles or corporate news pieces, for example. Understanding the biography of the executive will influence how you position your services and help you build rapport and establish a relationship with them.

## Rehearse your pitch

Rehearse your conversation with the executive. Think of any connection you have had with their biography. For example, perhaps you worked at a competitor company in the past; maybe you lived in the same country as them at some point. Also, consider the particular pressures associated with their role in the organization. For example:

- **Managing Director** – improving the profit and loss statement (P&L), increasing penetration of core business, expanding into new areas, meeting shareholder expectations

- **Marketing Director** – increasing revenues, finding cost-effective advertising, measuring the impact of campaigns

- **Human Resources Director** – attracting, selecting and retaining the best talent; implementing effective processes, improving employee engagement, preventing legal disputes.

## Use references

Tailor your experiences and references to the specific company. Most important to the executive will be your experience in their particular industry. Therefore, for each executive think about what work you have done in their sector, and then demonstrate the examples to them. Try to structure each example of previous work you have done in terms of:

- **Brief** – the problem or issue

- **Methodology** – the way you solved it

- **Outcome** – the positive impact this had on the business.

## Create your value proposition

A value proposition is a very important and well-used term in business. It provides a short summary of the value of doing business with you. To create your value proposition, consider the quantifiable benefits that you promise to deliver. This can be worked out by taking the benefits, costs and values that you can deliver (Value = benefits / costs).

## Write an elevator pitch

Although your preparation should leave you full of relevant information, unfortunately your client will not want to hear all the details of your knowledge. Do not overestimate the amount of interest they will have in you. People are mainly interested in themselves. Therefore, your pitch should be in the form of a short summary used to quickly and simply define your value proposition. This has become known as an elevator pitch, because it should be possible to describe it to a CEO whom you bump into in an elevator.

# Sales preparation

## Build rapport

The target executives will 'buy you' for both rational and irrational reasons. The rational is the most important and will be based on the business case that you present. The irrational will be based on how much rapport you have developed with the client. Do they like you? Are you a nice person? Did you brighten up their day or make it more miserable? Will they look forward to seeing you? To appeal to the irrational, it is necessary to be as polite, courteous and likeable to the client as possible.

## Go for the top

It may seem natural to assume that you should not bother the senior executives of a company with your services. They are, after all, extremely busy, serious professionals and you should instead approach lowly administrators. However, it is far more effective to target the most senior executives. Go in at the level of the CEO, or MD, and work your way down from there. At best, you will penetrate at the most important level of the organization; at worst, you will be passed on to deal with someone else. In this case, the person you are passed on to is much more likely to give you their attention because you have been referred to them by their boss.

## Leverage your network

Use the people that you have met in your life, or who are within the social circle of your family and friends. This is your network, and it is likely to include people who can help you to sell yourself more successfully. These people know you well and therefore have more rapport with you (the irrational), which makes them much more likely to 'buy you' and help you sell to others. Consider your network as:

- Friends

- Friends of friends

- Family

- Family friends

- Former colleagues

- Current customers

- People who attended your school or university (known as Alumni, this is particularly powerful at business school level and in the US)

- Acquaintances you have made both professionally and socially.

Business is based on relationships and networking. The better you are at networking the more likely you are to be successful. Therefore, take every opportunity you can to network and network with every person you meet. A useful tool in networking is to try to help the other person professionally. You can often do this by connecting them with someone else from your network, so that they can help them with what they want to achieve. This will create reciprocity, as this person then feels a desire to return the favour, and will help you in return. A truly great networker will create a thriving support system of professional favours being granted and returned.

## Get data

Outside of your social and professional network, the business world can seem like a giant and faceless bureaucracy. Finding out the name of the right person to talk to, and then getting to talk to them, can be very difficult. For example, if you telephone most established companies, the receptionist will tell you they operate 'a no-name policy', meaning that unless you know the name of the person you wish to speak to, they will not connect you to anyone.

None the less, it is possible to get access to the names, contact details and data you require. For example, in the United Kingdom, the names, titles, company names, as well as other information (which sometimes includes the financial details of limited companies), are officially recorded at Companies House. This data is sold by Companies House to data providers such as www.onesource.com. Therefore, if you subscribe to such a data provider, you can find out all the information of millions of executives and companies in order to begin approaching them.

## Structure a sales call

1. **Name and company** – Give your full name and company name so the client knows who they are dealing with.

2. **Do you have a moment to speak?** – Finding out if someone has time to speak to you is common courtesy. The client may be in the middle of working on an important project and should not be expected to drop everything because you have called. If they do not have time, you can ask for a specific time to call back. Make sure you do call back at this time, as this proves you are reliable.

3. **Elevator pitch** – Give your pitch as succinctly as possible, speaking clearly so that the executive can follow each point.

4. **Value proposition** – Highlight the benefits of what you are selling. Research shows that you should mirror the speech patterns of the person to whom you are talking. So, if you call a trader at a bank and they speak quickly, you should also speak quickly. If you call a Human Resources Director at a charity and they speak slowly and carefully, you should do the same.

5. **References** – Support the value proposition with real references to people and companies that have benefited from you in the past. Ideally, use examples from the same industry. Using the reference of a competitor is the most powerful, as this gives you credibility in your industry sector. It is also another incentive for an executive to talk to you in order to gain competitive intelligence.

6. **Could this be of interest to the company?** – Try to get the executive to talk to you. The more they talk the better. This will provide you with more information on what they need you to help with, while also building an affinity between you. From a practical point of view, it will mean that they have invested more time in you, and they are therefore more likely to continue that investment.

7. **When is convenient for you to meet and discuss?** – Meeting in person enables you to build a strong personal relationship with the executive. These people can then become a useful part of your existing network. It is also more likely that you can 'upsell' or complete a larger deal in person.

## Structuring an email

On the other hand, technological advances mean that many of the aspects of a face-to-face meeting are now available remotely. The benefit of working remotely is that you can achieve a higher volume of interactions. For example, a personalized mass email can present your value proposition to thousands of people in a few hours.

Email is a primary form of communication in the modern world. It is also one of the most powerful sales tools. Quite simply, people can read, and a brief, succinct and coherent email is an excellent vehicle for a sales pitch. But there are some ground rules to follow when structuring your email pitch:

1. **Dear (First Name)** – An email has to be personalized to be effective. This shows it is not simply spam and that the person has been targeted for a reason.

2. **I would like to present** – Summarize your value proposition and pitch it in one sentence. This enables a busy professional to scan the first line of the email and understand exactly what you want from them.

3. **An opportunity to (Company Name)** – Presenting the opportunity to a Company Name means it is less likely for it to be discarded. The offer becomes not just for that individual, but for the whole company. Is the executive able to discard it on behalf of the whole company? Perhaps they should share it with relevant colleagues? If the email is shared, it is a great benefit for you. An email shared by a colleague is more likely to be considered carefully. It also means more people become aware of you and what you are offering.

4. **The opportunity draws on resource X, it follows process X, and it is takes X amount of time** – Elaborate on the one-sentence pitch you gave in the first line of the email. Add three more clear sentences on the resource, process and time expectations of the client.

5. **Examples of recent projects for clients include** – Give three examples of similar projects you have done in the client's industry.

6. **A presentation with further information is attached** – Attach a comprehensive presentation for those who would perhaps like to find out more about your proposition.

7. **I am available to provide assistance or meet and discuss** – This is a sign of courtesy and shows that you are willing to provide a professional service that will meet the needs

of the client. It may also lead to a face-to-face meeting or teleconference, which is a highly important stage in sales.

8. **Add all contact details** – Add your contact details including email, telephone with international dialling code, and company website. It is also a good idea to add your mobile number so that you don't miss any calls back.

9. **Add credibility to your signature** – If you have postgraduate qualifications, or if your company has won any awards, add them to your email signature. This helps build your credibility and it is free advertising.

## Pre-meeting preparation

Despite the digital revolution, the business meeting remains a place where billions of dollars of revenues change hands every year. Whether it is a client meeting, an internal team meeting, or a job interview, performing well at meetings is crucial to success in business. In 2010, the Cranfield School of Management completed a study of 800 established sales professionals. They found out that just one simple behaviour increased sales significantly: pre-meeting preparation.

1. Before the meeting send an email confirmation, or an electronic invitation confirming the meeting, as early as possible to all involved.

2. Carry out market research on the company and executives using the techniques discussed on page 38.

3. Canvass people you know who have knowledge of the sector, company or client in advance for advice. Use this

information to begin forming key messages to communicate in the meeting.

4.  Diligently work on anything that has been asked of you. Respond to any requests for information. Bring a presentation on your company. Try to anticipate anything else that the client may find useful.

5.  Plan an agenda for the meeting.

## Example

### Meeting Agenda

Location:_____

Attendees: _____

Date: _____

Start and end time: _____

1.  Introductions – (insert: Client Name, My Name),
    10 minutes

2.  Briefing of project – (insert: Client Name),
    10 minutes

3.  Proposed project methodology – (insert: My Name),
    10 minutes

4.  Questions & Answers – (insert: Client Name, My Name),
    10 minutes

5.  Agreement on next steps – (insert: Client Name, My Name),
    10 minutes

6. Arrive 10–15 minutes early for the meeting, so that you are calm and have not had to rush to get there. Give a summary of what is going to be talked about and briefly go over the points of the meeting.

7. If you are in a sales meeting, take notes on everything the client says. This will give you a full understanding of the client's needs that you can refer back to later.

8. Following the meeting, write up your notes and store them, and then send a summary to all attendees, highlighting the key points discussed and the next steps to be taken.

## Follow up

Following up is essential to selling and to making things happen. Never be pushy, but politely and courteously prompt people into action. Busy professionals have many priorities and you will need to remind and prod them towards your objectives. If they reject your offer, be gracious in defeat and politely thank them for their consideration, leaving the door open for another opportunity in the future.

## Achieve high volume

Consider how you can reach as many of your target executives as possible. Success in sales requires great volume. For example, many sales organizations work on the principle that from 100 calls they will win one new client. This means that they have 1 per cent success rate, and in order to grow the business they need to increase the volume of calls.

Consider, faced with this business model, how you would build sales at this type of business. Perhaps you could hire more salespeople? Or use email to contact thousands more people? Maybe you could invest in training the salespeople so that the success rate moves to 2 per cent? Achieving the right results and a high enough volume could mean the difference between success and failure for your business.

## Client Relationship Management (CRM)

Record everything you do. During your life, you can build a database of thousands of contacts. We developed 20,000 contacts in our jobs, so when we launched our business we already had a supporting network. If you do manage to achieve high volume in approaching people, you will have many contacts. Remembering so many people's names, the interactions with each contact and the details of each deal becomes very difficult indeed. However, in order to be effective you need to remember all these details if you want to make deals happen. Therefore, record every single interaction you have on a Client Relationship Management (CRM) system. This can be done on Excel, but we recommend using an online provider, such as www.salesforce.com, which can store your contacts in the cloud so that you can access them anywhere in the world.

## Case study:
## Warren Buffett and the importance
## of personal preparation

There are few clearer examples of the benefits of personal preparation than the success of Warren Buffett. With an estimated wealth of $44 billion, Warren Buffett is one of the wealthiest men in the world. He acquired his fortune through a unique investment

# BUFFETT'S PREPARATION

Fundamentally, rather than trying to play the market, Warren Buffett's approach involves viewing the investment in a stock in the same way as investment in a business.

**The investment is made at a good price** – With a business, investors try to negotiate the best price possible. Likewise, Buffett invests only when Mr Market offers an attractive price following sharp falls in price, and within the margin of safety.

**The investment is long term** – With a business, investors generally aim for profits over the long term rather than immediate gains. In the same way, Buffett takes a long-term approach by investing in sound businesses over a long period of time, instead of following the schizophrenic trends of the market.

**The business is well managed** – With a business, investors consider the experience and approach of the managers. Buffett adopts a similar approach when looking at investing in a stock, and examines the management's approach to areas such as investing profits back into the business.

savvy that has earned him the nickname the 'Oracle of Omaha'. Today, he is regarded as one of the most successful stock market investors in history.

## What were his influences?

Born in 1930, Warren Buffett is the son of an American stockbroker who became a congressman. Warren became interested in finance as a young boy, and, as he grew, was particularly inspired by a book

**The business attempts to avoid debt** – With a business, investors would consider the risks associated with large debts. Buffett takes an analogous approach in investing in stocks. Therefore, he does not invest in companies with too much debt (sometimes called 'Leverage'), which can affect interest rates and reduce cash flow.

**The business has high returns** With a business, investors aim for reasonable Return On Investment. Buffett looks at the rate of return on investments in stocks. A rate of return means that if I invest £1,000 and my share price increases to £1,100 a year later, then I achieve a 10 per cent rate of return. Buffett estimates the average rate of return of US companies at approximately 11 per cent, so he looks for companies that have – and are demonstrating – higher returns to invest in.

**The business has a competitive edge** – investors consider a business that is doing something exceptional as an attractive proposition. In the same way, Buffett prefers to invest in well-known brands, such as Coca-Cola and Gillette, rather than 'commodity' companies that are not distinguishable from competitors except on price. These well-known brands provide something unique and therefore have a competitive advantage.

called *The Intelligent Investor* by Ben Graham. In this book, and its predecessor *Security Analysis*, Graham developed investment principles that shaped the business mind of Warren Buffett.

## Intrinsic business value

Graham came up with a principle of 'intrinsic business value' in order to illustrate how sensible investments are based on the basic value of a business, rather than the current view of the market. He used a parable about an investor known as 'Mr Market'.

## Mr Market

Mr Market is an imaginary eccentric business partner who offers to buy or sell you shares for different prices throughout the day. This presents an opportunity to make a profit, by buying when the prices fall sharply, and selling when the price rises substantially. You can confirm the price is too high or low by using an external benchmark such as the rate of return on government bonds. Making your investments in line with this rate provides you with a 'margin of safety'.

Buffett used these preparatory techniques to make some of the most successful investments in recent history.

A good example comes from 1988, when he assessed Coca-Cola as being a good investment opportunity. He consequently began a frenzy of buying stock in the company, spending $1.02 billion and accumulating 7 per cent of Coca-Cola. As a result of such investments, his company Berkshire Hathaway's share price rose from $2,600 to $80,000 in the 1990s.

By the early twenty-first century, Warren Buffett became the richest man in the world (interchanging places with Bill Gates, depending on the market). At the time of writing, Buffett is ranked as the third wealthiest man in the world by *Forbes* magazine.

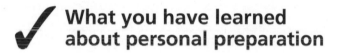

## What you have learned about personal preparation

In this chapter, you have learned that personal preparation is fundamental to success in business. You must prepare certain key items in order to sell yourself successfully. This preparation will enable you not only to fully understand the business you are involved in, but also to impress others with your professionalism and dedication.

# Step 3:
# Personal Presentation

'In the beginning it was just about
the business – now it's about the brand.'
**Sir Richard Branson**

## Why is personal presentation important?

When you look at the business world, you may feel small and uncompetitive in comparison to the giants of industry, the business gurus and investment dragons. However, those giants of industry may in fact be in debt and about to collapse (see top US investment bank Lehman Brothers, for example), and some of the investment dragons may really be on the verge of bankruptcy themselves.

Through personal presentation business people and organizations determine how the world sees them. When the business world looks at you, it can only see what you present. Business people such as Sir Richard Branson have used personal presentation to develop global brands and expand their personal fortunes.

# How this chapter will help you with personal presentation

*Learn to harness personal presentation, including:*

*Individual presentation:*
- *Dress for business*
- *Avoid preconceptions*
- *Write the perfect CV*

*Personal presentation the Branson way:*
- *Develop business based on your qualities and values*
- *Win support by giving back*
- *Face challenges*
- *Use your own profile to support your business*
- *Maintain a rational approach*
- *Do whatever it takes*
- *Experiment*
- *Expand out of a crisis*
- *Learn all the time*

# Individual presentation

## Dress for business

A general rule of business is that people like to do business with people who are already successful. (Think about it: would you rather hold a meeting with a well-known entrepreneur or an office tea boy?) It is possible to project an image of success through dressing for business. Making an effort in your appearance also shows that you respect the people you are meeting.

For a business situation, a suit, shirt and tie for a man should provide the foundation. A smart two-piece business suit is good for women, but there are other options too, as long as the outcome is smart and professional. Both sexes should carefully maintain personal grooming, with polished shoes, clean hair, nails manicured, etc. You should not take off your jacket when meeting someone, even if it is a hot day, unless they do so first.

Pay attention to the finer details, as these will be noticed by others and provide clues to your success. An elegant watch, a well-pressed shirt and a refined pair of shoes will set you above the rest. For the really discerning eye, a designer suit made from high-quality fabric will make even more of an impact. None the less, a suit is not necessarily the right outfit for all business environments. If you work in a creative industry, more casual clothes may be suitable. Research the suitable dress code for each situation and dress accordingly.

## Avoid preconceptions

Always be careful not to judge other people simply by the clothes they wear. Truly successful wealthy people have no need to conform to norms of wearing business suits.

This is another lesson we learned the hard way. We had a business meeting in the City of London, and were joined by a scruffy unkempt man with a ponytail, dressed in a pair of jeans and a T-shirt. He received disparaging looks from the other businessmen around and he was almost refused service at the bar. However, we noticed that the cigarette pack he was carrying had a picture of himself on it. He was, in fact, a celebrated entrepreneur and multimillionaire, who was probably the most successful person in the room.

---

**HINT BOX**

*Compliment*

*A compliment is a powerful way of making people feel good, like you more and be suggestible to whatever you are selling. Whenever you are impressed by something about someone, don't just think it, tell them. If they have developed a great company culture, comment on it. If they seem to fully understand their market, tell them how knowledgeable they are. Even tell them if they are wearing a nice tie. Making people feel good about themselves will mean that they also feel good about you.*

---

# Write the perfect CV

In today's business world, looking good on paper is just as crucial to selling yourself as looking good in person. The perfect CV is not an art form but a science, and one that can be perfected through the application of various rules and methods. It should be a reflection of your career to date, highlighting your most successful achievements, your progress and capabilities. Remember: your CV will reach your potential employer long before they get to meet you. In fact, it provides the basis for whether they decide to meet with you at all, and it is therefore hugely important.

It is often said that a recruiter will spend an average of eight seconds reviewing a CV, so it should be clear and easy to navigate. If they can't find the points they are looking for, they will put your CV to one side and carry on with the search.

Unless you have had a thirty-year career with lots of different jobs, then there is no reason for your CV to read like an essay and be twenty pages long. You should ideally be able to fit your CV on one or two pages only, no more than that.

## The core components of a CV

**Personal details** – Name / Contact Details / Do not include Age

**Work experience** – Start with the most recent position and work chronologically backwards. Here, you should include the name of the firm and a one-line description, such as: PrintCo – A UK-wide printing shop franchise with twenty stores, 100 employees and £20 million in turnover.

List your title and the location of the firm. Also provide a clear outline of the dates during which you worked at the company.

With regard to the content of your work experience, you must avoid simply reciting the job description that you had once applied to. Your future employer is concerned with the results that you achieved and the difference you made to the organization. Take out many of the mundane daily tasks that you were responsible for, saving the space for those three big achievements you had throughout your time at the company. These are the moments that should be on your CV and they should also follow the STAR Formula (see box below).

It is also worth remembering to use strong language in your work experience statement. Revisit your list of power verbs from page 151. Remember to talk about your achievements in the past tense so that it is obvious that these achievements have already been completed.

## STAR Formula

**Situation** – The company name and your title in the heading takes care of this.

**Task** – The activity you were responsible for – a marketing project for a new product or perhaps serving coffee at Starbucks.

**Action** – What did you do? 'Conducted in-depth market and customer research through focus groups and interviews that identified insights upon which to build a marketing strategy' *or* 'Maintained strong customer focus and positive attitude'.

**Result** – What was achieved through your actions? 'Resulting in a 40 per cent market penetration with product sales exceeding forecasts by 10 per cent' or 'Resulting in a customer feedback score of 90 per cent and recommendation for employee of the month three times in a row'.

Through using the STAR Formula, your statement becomes very powerful and your future employer has something tangible to speak to you about at an interview. Your statement can also help them understand how you approach challenges.

**List academic experience** – List your degree or postgraduate studies, as well as your A-levels and GCSEs if still relevant. As time passes, these will become less important and you will be able to reduce your academic section to simply your degrees.

**Other skills** – Here you should cite any languages that you speak and your level of competence, but only if you would be confident enough to use these language skills in the workplace. The ability to order a meal or a drink on holiday does not warrant a mention. Additionally, note any *relevant* computer skills. Generally, remember that the most important factor here is to only describe 'relevant' skill sets. The fact that you can swim 200 metres in five minutes is not of merit to most employers and should be omitted – unless applying to a job where this is a requirement.

**Interests** – It is in this section that you can show your potential employer that you have a personality. Here you can tell them – using one to four points – about something that makes you different. Statements like 'Climbed Mt Everest to raise money for UNICEF' should be first on your list, along with statements that show you have something unique outside of being the model professional. Should your statements read 'Passionate about film and wine' and this is true, then that is fine as well, however think about what else might make you stand out from the crowd just that little bit more.

**Reread and edit** – Finally, it is important that you tailor your CV to suit each job you apply for. There is no point applying for a finance position with a CV that describes your success in sales, or vice versa. Each time you use your CV it should have been amended to fit the specific position.

# Case study:
# Sir Richard Branson and personal presentation

Sir Richard Branson has risen from publishing a magazine at the tender age of sixteen to leading the Virgin Group, a conglomerate with a portfolio of more than 200 companies spanning dozens of countries and generating an annual operational turnover of $10 billion. He is a master of personal presentation and a resurgent symbol of British entrepreneurialism.

## Develop business based on your qualities and values

In a new and unique way, Sir Richard Branson has become the Virgin Brand. Coca-Cola is symbolized by its distinctive red branding; Apple by a half-eaten white fruit; but Virgin by its founder Sir Richard Branson. He is the role model for a new lifestyle in which a business expresses the personality of its founder. His values rest on five main pillars:

1. Value for money
2. Good quality
3. Brilliant customer service
4. Innovation
5. Competitive challenge and fun.

In the same way, your business can represent the business values that you developed in Step 1 (see pages 21–2). This means that you should only ever enter into a business if you truly believe in it. Ensure that your core values are reflected in all that you do.

## Win support by giving back

Caring about people (be it customers, employees or society at large) has always been one of Richard Branson's core values, which is well reflected in his business ventures. His European chain of health clubs, Virgin Active, offers customers the flexibility to pay as and when they use the facilities, rather than binding them to long-term contractual agreements. A similar strategy, taken up by Virgin Mobile in the US, attracted about 4 million customers. He achieved this by offering pre-paid phone cards primarily to the younger generation who could not afford costly long-term contracts.

Branson has also initiated a number of ventures for looking after more vulnerable people, such as student support centres (now under the umbrella of charity Virgin Unite). Likewise, Virgin staff receive cut-price access to Virgin services, such as cable television, and discounted nights at Branson's exclusive nightclubs. Branson has always made clear the emphasis he puts on caring about people. As he said in an interview with Jane Pauley in 2005:

> If you're good with people ... and you really care, genuinely care, about people then I'm sure we could find a job for you at Virgin. The companies that look after their people are the companies that do really well. I'm sure we'd like a few other attributes, but that would be the most important one.

## Face challenges

From his early childhood, Branson was taught a unique sense of purpose. His mother would give him challenges, such as sending the twelve-year-old Richard to cycle to Bournemouth and back. He was given no water, but told he should find it on the way: Bournemouth was fifty miles away from his home.

As a young man, Branson had a great passion for taking up the most challenging of adventures, which included breaking the world record for sailing across the Atlantic in a 99-foot super Maxi yacht, and making transatlantic crossings in a hot-air balloon. His craving for challenges and risk-taking is captured in his own words: 'The balloons only have one life and the only way of finding out whether they work is to attempt to fly around the world.'

## Use your own profile to support your business

Branson has been able to develop a leadership style that is unique to him, and the global market domination of the Virgin Group is a testimony of its success. He has also been prepared to use his own profile to raise media attention to support his business, as was the case when Virgin Air was in financial difficulty and in strong competition with British Airways. At the time, Branson used influence he had gained by befriending King Hussein of Jordan (during a hot-air balloon expedition) to reach an agreement with Saddam Hussein to free British hostages in Iraq. Amazingly, Branson personally flew to rescue the hostages in a Virgin plane, and returned to Britain triumphant, receiving exceptionally positive PR. Following this event, Branson believes that British Airways became so concerned about his popularity that they planned a coordinated 'dirty tricks' campaign to damage his personal image and regain competitive advantage.

## Maintain a rational approach

Behind all of his business decisions, Branson has always maintained very strong foresight, rational thinking and astute business acumen. An ideal example of the strategic growth of his business ventures is his successive expansion from mail order records to video distribution. At the very outset, he expanded the mail order record system to a retail records business. This opened up business opportunities in record production, which in turn led to the opening of a music publishing company.

## Do whatever it takes

Branson has been distinguished by an uninhibited ambition and confidence, which has seen him ignore restraints and go straight for what his business needs. It is true that he may be willing to 'bend the truth', and he is certainly willing to approach whoever is necessary.

For example, one time he heard that potential buyers of luxury property would be provided with free travel and accommodation. Wanting to take advantage of this (especially since he wanted to take a lover on a romantic break at the time), Branson told an estate agent that he was considering buying an island in the British Virgin Islands. Arrangements were made and he viewed an island that was valued at £3 million – this was over ten times the £100,000 Branson had available at the time. None the less, he decided to put in this shockingly low offer and was subsequently kicked out of his complimentary luxury villa. Some months later, however, the seller badly needed the cash and Branson managed to buy the island for only £180,000. Today, Necker Island is one of the most exclusive holiday destinations in the world, and it is worth hundreds of millions of pounds.

## Experiment

Branson has always prioritized swift action to situations, rather than spending time and money speculating on the possible outcomes and potential losses. This might defy popular management theories, but if it is backed by foresight and rational thinking it can earn immediate results. For example, once, while travelling in an aeroplane, Branson wanted to interact with a pretty girl seated in the next aisle but was instead stuck in his cramped seat, away from her, for the duration of the journey. This made him think and led to the introduction of the Stand Up Bars in Virgin cabins.

On another occasion, his wife's manicurists suggested introducing manicure services as part of the Virgin in-flight customer care package. Sir Richard immediately picked up the idea (without caring too much about market research and viability study) and integrated it with his core customer service offers. As a result, the Virgin crew now boasts around 700 beauty therapists on its staff.

## Expand out of a crisis

Despite the fame Sir Richard Branson has received for his success in business today, it has not always been this way. In 1980, Virgin was headed for a £1 million loss and Branson's business partner at the time, Nik Powell, was worried enough to consider selling his shares.

However, during this difficult financial period Branson did not cut back staff or assets, but instead purchased two nightclubs – Kensington Roof Gardens and G.A.Y Club. The extra £1 million liability that this purchase created was considered by Powell to plunge them into more financial trouble. However, in the longer term these nightclubs greatly increased their value and added glamour and fun to the Virgin brand.

This approach has characterized Sir Richard Branson's success. When facing a crisis, he did not contract his businesses or make redundancies. Instead, he expanded out of it. This ambitious principle is one of the secrets of Branson's success.

## Learn all the time

Richard Branson has been a lifelong learner and all his experiences – business or personal, successful or disastrous – have taught him invaluable lessons that have been fundamental to his personal and professional growth. Now an honorary PhD, Branson had aspired to be a journalist at the outset of his career, but ended up being one of the most successful entrepreneurs of his generation. He has spoken insightfully about this, in a truly Richard Branson style: 'The reason I went into business originally was not because I thought I could make a lot of money, but because the experiences I had personally with businesses were dire and I wanted to create an experience that I and my friends could enjoy.'

Sir Richard is said to be deeply inspired by Nelson Mandela, President Carter and Barack Obama, but still maintains a personal presentation that is unique only to him.

# ✓ What you have learned about personal presentation

In this chapter, you have learned the importance of success to image, and image to success. Through personal presentation, you can project an image of achievement that becomes self-perpetuating. You can also use personal presentation to convey professionalism, competence and experience through business tools such as your résumé. Sir Richard Branson shows how you can take personal presentation even further by expressing your personality through your business, and becoming the living breathing representation of a brand.

# Step 4:
# Communication

'Communication works for those
who work at it.'
**John Powell**

## Why communicate?

The ability to communicate with others is one of the most important skills in business. It is the means by which we convey, convince, dispel objections and unite. It is an art form that requires constant work.

We have all heard of and witnessed the power of great communication through exemplary leaders such as Winston Churchill, Nelson Mandela and Barack Obama. All of these leaders were not naturally gifted with the power of great rhetoric and performance, but were able to hone their skills through years of practice and preparation. Great communication can have a hugely positive impact – from having the power to move nations or motivating a company's workforce to getting a client to sign the required contract.

In today's technological minefield, we are confronted with a multitude of options that enable us to get our message across, and each one comes with certain protocols that can help us to achieve our goals more efficiently.

## Hear what isn't being said

The Greek philosopher Epictetus said: 'We have two ears and one mouth so that we can listen twice as much as we speak.' This message is as true today as it was back in c. AD 100. The art of communication begins with the art of listening. In order to truly communicate with someone, it is important that you understand where they are coming from and what it is they want. As the management guru Peter Drucker once implied, the greatest thing in communication is to hear what isn't being said. This requires certain characteristics, such as patience and a willingness to understand what is being asked of you. It is by this act of taking a genuine interest that you will become truly engaged and engaging. This in itself will make the person with whom you wish to communicate more inclined to open up and express their true desires, concerns and abilities.

## Active listening

If you want to absorb more than the usual 25 to 50 per cent of incoming messages that the client or interviewer is transmitting, it is worthwhile investing the time to practise becoming an active listener. Active listening can be achieved through repeating the processes discussed in this chapter. Remember that active listening can make the difference between picking and not picking up key signals that could determine whether you close a deal.

# How this chapter will help with your communication

*Learn important facts about communication, including:*

*Verbal, non-verbal, written and visual communication:*

- *Body language, spoken language and mirroring*
- *Shake hands firmly*
- *Have good posture*
- *Demonstrate that the message is getting through*
- *Confirm you heard the key points*
- *Understanding your audience*
- *Structuring your discussion*
    - *Deductive reasoning*
    - *Inductive reasoning*
- *Excellence in presentation*
- *The written word*

# Verbal, non-verbal, visual and written communication

When conducting a business meeting, or in an interview situation, there are several non-verbal ways of encouraging a positive response.

## Body language, spoken language and mirroring

Look at the other person's body language – see for example how they are sitting, and if they move their arms and hands a lot – and notice the type of spoken language they are using. Then try to mirror these. Through this act you will begin to create similarities in the listener's mind. It is important not to overdo this, though. Make sure you do it subtly, otherwise you run the risk of being seen as sarcastic or false.

## Shake hands firmly

If you are delivering the message in person, remember to give a firm handshake to those who are in easy reach of you. This is not to say that you should crush their hands, but rather grip with a confident assertiveness. There has also been somewhat of a double standard, providing a limp or loose handshake when greeting a woman. This is advised against, and whilst you should look not to grip too hard, a firm grasp here shows a belief in equality and a trust in the other person's abilities. It is important when delivering in person that you seem passionate about what you are saying, and this can be achieved through your body language. It is estimated that some 68 per cent of the message that we transmit comes not from our words but from our body language.

## Have good posture

When you are delivering a message, ensure that your body is upright. This applies when either standing or sitting. It can also be of great advantage to use your hands. A prime of example of someone who uses powerful gesticulation is former Prime Minister Tony Blair. He would effectively spread his arms with palms upwards, transmitting an appearance of transparency and openness. Another useful tool is what has been coined the 'power thumbs'. This is in place of pointing, which is often seen as aggressive and intrusive. Power thumbs can be used by holding a gripped fist with your thumbs slightly extended, which you then move up and down forcefully to the beat of each point.

## Demonstrate that the message is getting through

Through the act of nodding or shaking your head at appropriate moments, the speaker will know that you are engaged in the conversation and again feel more comfortable with you. Facial expressions that demonstrate you understand the message delivered will further prove that you are listening. A way to get the person to continue speaking is to offer tones of encouragement. As you verbally agree with them or respond, they will then continue to elaborate on their message, giving you further information to use in constructing your response.

## Confirm you heard the key points

Once the speaker has finished, you want to make sure that you have understood the key aspects of their message. Repeat what you have heard them say in sentences such as, 'If I could just confirm' or 'If I have understood you correctly'. If your deductions are correct, you will then be able to build your response more closely to target their points.

With these actions complete, it is now your turn to respond, and in doing so there are some important principles that you must adhere to, the first of which is how to understand your audience.

## Understanding your audience

If you are discussing a message with the CEO of a company, then the subjects that will be of pivotal importance to them are likely to be very different from those of the average employee. The key concerns of the Buying Manager will not be the same as those of the Marketing Manager, and a lack of awareness around this point will lead you to convey the wrong messages, which will possibly lose you the sale or job. Before you begin any conversation, just as is stated in the previous chapter, you must find out who your audience is and what they can do.

Each person will have a different level of authority and capabilities, and as such there is no point in asking them to do or agree to something that is outside of their remit. This is also therefore a key part of your preparation as you must ensure that you are in fact speaking to the right person. You must identify the key decision maker who has the potential to say 'Yes' to whatever your desired outcome is.

You should also be aware of the following differences so that you adjust not only the content of your discussion but also the tone and language you use. As you listen to the speaker you will notice that they may use certain types of words and give clues away as to their own communication style. Scientists will use more language and phases based on facts and figures, while advertising executives will use a greater number of images and adjectives. You should therefore try to mirror this and use the same style of language as they do. As Irish dramatist William Butler Yeats said, 'Think like a wise man but communicate in the language of the people'. If presenting to a group, you should include this concept in your presentation. There is no point using images of a profit graph to a Finance Director who is only concerned with facts and figures of the true profit and loss report.

This point is also vital in developing the right pitch because the audience will be the deciding factor in how long you have. A busy company executive may only have a couple of minutes available as opposed to the full half an hour, and therefore it is essential that you can communicate your point in the time provided. In order to do this, it is key that you take on board the following point of how to structure your communication.

## Structuring your discussion

As we have already highlighted, there are no two people who are the same, and as such you must be flexible in your method of communication and prepare for each accordingly. You should always do your research before you meet someone, as stated in Step 2: Personal Preparation.

If you are dealing with those who are time-pressed, it is important that you put the key points of the message at the beginning of the conversation so that you are guaranteed to get these points across. With those who are more generous with their time, it is possible to build up to the key message with some background. However, if you did not know who you were talking to and were not aware of their time constraints, then you would not be able to structure your conversation to its optimum performance level.

Another point that is fundamental to structuring a discussion is about developing the right logical flow of the argument. Barbara Minto, the former Communications Director of McKinsey & Company (widely believed to be one of the most professional firms in the world), wrote a book called *The Pyramid Principle*. In this book, Minto explains – among other things – that there are two primary types of logical argument construction that should be used: 'Deductive' and 'Inductive' reasoning.

**Deductive reasoning** – Deductive reasoning should be used to convey simpler fact-based arguments. It should begin with one key thought which is your primary statement. If one was to take the example of someone looking to convince another of the merits of recycling, then the discussion might go as follows:

**Primary thought:** 'The environment is in trouble and recycling is an effective way to save it.'

This statement is now the key point to which all of your following statements go in to support. From here, you can now build a base of secondary supporting points with tertiary sub-points that further reinforce the argument to which it belongs. Examples of this can be seen below:

- **Secondary thought 1**: 'Recycling saves land.'
- **Tertiary thought 1.1**: '1 million acres of land a year could be saved through reducing the amount of landfills used.'
- **Tertiary thought 1.2**: '150 acres of land could be saved each year through building fewer factories to build extra products which would not be needed if we recycled.'
- **Secondary thought 2:** 'Recycling saves energy.'

- **Tertiary thought 2.1:** '100 billion kilowatts of electricity could be saved through recycling products rather than having to manufacture them from scratch again.'
- **Tertiary thought 2.2:** 'And so ...'

This can make for a very strong argument and is especially useful when dealing with people who require fact-based points in order to be convinced.

**Inductive reasoning** – The second method of inductive reasoning can also be useful, particularly in the absence of solid facts. This however does leave it susceptible to more cynical audiences. This type of logic could be explained through the example of a passenger looking to convince a colleague of selecting one means of transport over another. The conversation would still begin with a key statement to which all of your following statements will go to support.

**Primary thought:** 'Taking the train will get us there before taking the plane.'

From here, you begin with a statement about the current situation:

'The train takes longer than the plane. However, the train is due to arrive before the plane.

This should then be followed up with an observation:

'I have checked the time reports and there are currently delays at the airport. It also takes a longer time to get into town from the airport.'

Finally, an action with supporting points should be made:

'We can therefore arrive thirty minutes earlier if we get the train, as there is no need for a taxi into town and there are no delays. We will also be able to avoid check-in and passport queues.'

It will be up to you to decide the receptiveness of your audience and the weight of the facts available to you. Once you have decided on your structure, you can then begin to work on the format of your delivery. Here again, there are multiple formats that further add to the complications of ensuring the optimum results.

## Excellence in presentation

Steve Jobs – widely considered to be one of the most effective PowerPoint writers in the world – outlines a number of principles that should be followed. These include limiting the number of words you have on each slide. Jobs explains that the word count should be limited to fifty words maximum, but this does not include extra text such as sources (which should be a prerequisite whenever quoting sources or data). This practice will help you to be more concise and focus on the core messages.

This must be accompanied by general common sense rules, such as using a clear font so that everyone can read it without any complications. Another key point is to make sure that the headline is clear. Your headline should summarize the entire content of the slide and the reason for its existence. One way to think about this is: if your whole presentation were to be read by a very busy CEO, could he/she read the headlines of each slide only and still understand the key points? Would he/she be able to take away the key points and recommendations? If this is possible, then you have achieved your goal.

Throughout the presentation, it is also of great use to remember the old adage 'a picture speaks a thousand words'. Whilst this is not possible for all slides or presentations, it is often a very useful tool in getting across common themes – and it can also be useful in introducing an element of humour into the presentation. Most importantly though, research has shown that by combining a powerful verbal message with an image, there is a 75 per cent greater chance of your message being recalled than when using words alone.

Should you be one of the many who suffer from nerves, and as a result speaks too fast or forgets their words, don't worry. These issues disappear with practice. If you speak too fast, then practise speaking slowly. Buy a newspaper that is more verbose perhaps than your usual read. Then practise reading an article out loud slowly each day. Remember to speak slowly and to physically force yourself to slow down. Over time this slower tone will become natural when presenting.

Another tip is to take a moment to yourself before the presentation to slow down your breathing. Hold your hands to your mouth and practise breathing in and out slowly into your hands ten times. Follow this with three large deep breaths and then breathe back into your hands ten times. This will gradually bring your heartbeat down, making you feel calmer, and make it easier for you to deliver the presentation.

There is also no shame in taking notes up on stage with you. The key here though is to ensure that each of the cards has a maximum of three key words on it. These words are to act as prompts and remind you of the points you are going to make. They are not to be used as scripts and you need to be careful when using them to carry on engaging with your audience and maintaining eye contact with them.

## The written word

The growth in email communication has created a whole new range of issues and potential pitfalls (see also 'Structuring an email' on page 44). The most common of these can be avoided by simply structuring your communications more efficiently, using the tactics outlined on page 45. A clear opening sentence explaining the reasoning for your communication can save paragraphs of waffle.

Well-defined paragraphs will make it easier for the recipient to digest and understand the information. It is also advisable to use bullet points to identify lists and key points of action or points that require a response. Furthermore, it is vital to convey the correct impression by only using full words; do not get drawn into using the language of SMS. There is also no need for spelling mistakes, especially as every email program now comes with spelling and grammar checks.

However, the most important point regarding email communication is to remember that digital is for ever. Once the send button has been pressed, it will be recorded for the duration of time on some file within the ether for ever. As the author of *Think and Grow Rich*, Napoleon Hill, once said, 'If you must speak ill of another, do not speak it, write it in the sand near the water's edge'. This advice certainly applies to communication in the digital age … what you write will be with you for ever – so choose your words with care.

# Case study:
# Oprah Winfrey and communication

Oprah Winfrey has used exceptional communication skills to become the first African American billionaire and one of the most powerful women in the world.

Born into poverty in 1954, Oprah experienced severe child abuse, but overcame these setbacks by cultivating skills as a public speaker, beginning with reciting the Bible. As a teenager, she won an oratory competition and a scholarship to Tennessee State University where she studied communication. By the age of eighteen, she was putting her education into practice, with a position as a news anchor before hosting the TV show *Chicago AM*. Her popularity and unique communication style saw the show become hugely popular – so much so that it was renamed *The Oprah Winfrey Show* and syndicated across America.

Oprah's communication style revolutionized the chat show format, with unique elements including:

- Empathy – Complete absorption in the communicative interactions, conveyed by attentive listening. This was particularly apparent in a defining moment in popular culture when in 1993 Oprah interviewed Michael Jackson. In the most watched interview in television history, Jackson – the most famous man in the world – opened up about missing out on a normal childhood.

- Confidence – Any trace of untrustworthiness or lack of belief is removed by totally confident verbal delivery. This was shown in an interview with George Bush when

Oprah led the former president to discuss some of his most difficult decisions.

- Openness – Sharing her own experiences to draw the audience in and make them feel connected and involved. This was most strikingly shown when, during a programme covering sexual molestation, Oprah cried and confessed on television that she had been raped as a child. The impact of this approach has been so great that the *Wall Street Journal* coined the term 'Oprahfication' to describe public confession as a form of therapy.

- Frankness – Her personal credibility has been enhanced further by her honest style, which has included asking hard questions and on occasions challenging others. This was clear when Oprah questioned James Frey, author of *A Million Little Pieces*, on television, regarding inconsistencies in his book.

- Authenticity – Her body language perfectly expresses words to provide a consistency that conveys a sense of authenticity. Oprah has had many authentic moments on television, including meeting her sister for the first time.

By the age of thirty-two Oprah was a millionaire with a TV show at the top of the ratings. She went on to become an exceptional businesswoman with interests in publishing, including two magazines, *The Oprah Magazine* and *O at Home*. The Oprah radio station was launched in 2006 with a reported $55 million contract. The website Oprah.com averages more than 70 million page views and more than 6 million users per month. Most ambitiously, in

2009, Oprah launched her own television network OWN, available to 70 million homes. These media interests provide Oprah with a 360-degree presence, and the ability to engage with her audience through a number of different media. On 25 May 2011, the last *Oprah Winfrey Show* aired on television, but she continues to exert influence behind the scenes through her network. By 2011 her earnings were estimated at $290 million per year, with an overall fortune of $2.7 billion. The power of Oprah's communicative skills was noted by US President Barack Obama, who stated, 'she may be the most influential woman in the country'.

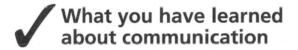

## ✓ What you have learned about communication

In summary, the ability to communicate effectively will be fundamental to your success in selling yourself. It is by no means the birthright of anyone to be naturally gifted in this skill – however, it is one that can be practised and learned to perfection (as was recently demonstrated in the Oscar-winning film *The King's Speech*).

If you are to truly succeed though, you must understand who your audience are, what it is they want to hear, and how they want it to be delivered. This must all be part of your preparation. This will then allow you to decide on the appropriate structure and medium through which to communicate. Your body language, tone and inclination should all convey the confidence that you and your message deserve. This should be backed up by the effective use of tools that facilitate your transmission of the message.

# Step 5:
# Empathy

'The end result of kindness is that it
draws people to you.'
**Anita Roddick**

## Why is empathy important?

Selling yourself is not actually only about you. If you want to persuade
and influence people to buy into your idea, product or service, you
must first understand *them*. Even exceptionally smart people who have
had an excellent education, possess a good sense of humour and high
levels of energy – in other words, those prone to success – can fail if
they miss the 'soft' skills needed for becoming a top leader.

This is a principle that was not lost on former British Prime Minister
Tony Blair when he represented London's successful bid for the 2012
Olympics:

> In the course of the meetings, I learned yet again how
> important it is to listen as well as talk. Knowing when to shut
> up is one of the most vital rules in life, never mind in politics.
> Basically, most people are psychological itinerants in search of
> someone who wants to hear about them, who is interested in

what they have to say, and who will regard what they say as both sage and stimulating. This applies at any level. In fact, the more elevated the level, the truer it is. In most of my meetings with other leaders – I would listen or ask them questions to get them talking, so that I could listen. A good meeting is one where you have listened more than you have spoken. (Tony Blair, *A Journey*, 2010)

As the pace of globalization increases, work is more and more based on teamwork. If you want to be successful as a person, seller, leader or employee, then you need more than education and even experience; you need cognitive, emotional and physical abilities to, as Daniel Goleman put it in his book, *Social Intelligence*, 'do more than sympathize with people around [you]' … you need to use your 'knowledge to improve [your] companies in subtle, but important ways'.

## How this chapter will help you with empathy

*Learn to empathize and find out about:*

- *Developing Emotional Intelligence (EQ)*
- *The business results of empathy*
- *How empathy works*
- *Empathy in practice*
- *Four steps to improve your empathy skills*

# What is empathy?

The word 'empathy' comes from both Latin and Greek, and can be translated as 'to see through' and 'the eye of the other'. It can also be defined as the ability to read other people. Other definitions mention identifying with the other person or their situation. 'Identifying' implies more than a cognitive understanding; it means that based on your own experiences, you can recall some of those same feelings. Therefore, empathy skills are: listening, attending to the needs and wants of others, and building relationships.

> **HINT BOX**
>
> *Empathy: the ability to 'see through the eye of the other', to feel what the other person is feeling, to put yourself in the other person's shoes.*

## Developing Emotional Intelligence (EQ)

Emotional Intelligence (EQ) is the ability to be aware of one's own emotions and others' feelings, to differentiate between the two, and to be able to use this understanding in order to guide other people's thinking and behaviour. It is more than being emotional or controlling your emotions; it is about understanding when emotions will be helpful and when not.

Research by Boyatzis and McKee in 2001 has shown that high levels of emotional intelligence are correlated to higher levels of information-sharing, trust, healthy risk-taking and learning, while low levels of emotional intelligence lead to fear and anxiety. Furthermore, Daniel Goleman in his books *Emotional Intelligence: Why It Can Matter*

*More than IQ* and *Working with Emotional Intelligence*, suggested that people with high levels of EQ are more likely to get to the top of corporations. To Goleman, emotional intelligence matters twice as much as other technical or analytical skills for star performance. This was evident recently, when US President Barack Obama used 'empathy' as one of his criteria for selecting a nominee to the Supreme Court: 'We need somebody who's got the heart, the empathy, to recognize what it's like to be a young teenage mom.'

According to Goleman, there are five component skills that build emotional intelligence, namely:

- **Self-awareness** – Understanding yourself. Understanding your own emotions, strengths and weaknesses – and how these impact on others – is essential to understanding the feelings of other people.

- **Self-management** – Managing your emotions and impulses. You do not only understand your emotions, but you also express them carefully, showing a high level of judgement and control.

- **Self-motivation** – The ability to remain focused on goals despite setbacks. Strong inner drive will make it hard to break your spirit or thwart your confidence.

- **Social awareness** – Understanding others. You possess compassion and understand human nature, which enables you to connect emotionally with others.

- **Social skills** – Managing others. The ability to deal with problems without allowing your own or others' negative feelings to interfere.

## The business results of empathy

Empathy is not only important in relationships; there are numerous studies that link empathy to business results. There seems to be a high correlation between empathy and increased sales, productivity and organizational performance. Empathy is also particularly critical to leadership skills.

Indeed, empathy facilitates the creation of trust and without empathy people will lack sufficient flexibility for change, and won't be able to work well in teams and sell themselves. EQ is a skill required for all kind of jobs:

- Managers and leaders need high EQ to represent the organization to the public, to interact well with people within and outside the organization, and to set the tone for employee morale. Leaders with empathy are able to understand their employees' needs and provide them with constructive feedback.

- Sales people require empathic ability to gauge a customer's mood, and the interpersonal skill to decide when to speak about a product and when to keep quiet.

- Painters or professional tennis players, for example, need to intelligently manage their emotions in order to achieve self-discipline and motivation.

## How empathy works

We should, then, cultivate empathy. But how does empathy work? Is it a process of thinking or of emotion? Is it a feeling, a thought, or an action? Well, it actually includes both a physiological reaction ('affective sharing' – see below) and a cognitive component. Some authors have suggested that other cognitive skills, such as self-awareness and emotion regulation, are also critical components of empathy.

The four components of empathy identified by J. Decety and Y. Moriguchi in an article in *BioPyschoSocial Medicine* in 2007, are as follows:

1.  **Mental flexibility and perspective taking** – The cognitive ability to understand how another person feels and what they might be thinking, and also to imagine what it would be like to experience the world from their position.

2.  **Affective sharing** – The 'reflection' of another person's observable experience, feeling physically connected with the other person as though their emotions were contagious. It happens when you laugh when someone else laughs, or when you are sad after seeing another person cry. What is the rationale behind immediate and instinctive reaction to other people's experiences? How do we understand their feelings in that particular moment or situation?

    One study in 2009 used fMRI imaging to observe the brains of individuals. They watched videos of people describing highly emotional events in their lives. The researchers found heightened activity in two specific areas of the brain: one that 'mirrored' the storytellers being watched on the videotape, and another that appeared to be responsible for cognitively processing and articulating a description of the storytellers' feelings. The one that mirrored the storytellers is called the mirror neuron system, which creates an automatic mirroring of activities associated with feelings, such as facial expressions. This system contains a special type of brain cells, or neurons, that become active when a person consciously imitates someone else's actions. For example, imagine you are sitting at a café enjoying your latte and watching the people at the other tables. All of a sudden, the woman in front of you splashes hot tea on her hand. You immediately 'feel' the pain and empathize with her.

3. **Self-awareness** – The ability to differentiate between the 'self' experience and the other person's experience. Mirroring can be very powerful, leading to identification between the self and the other.

4. **Emotion regulation** – In order to counterbalance the effect of mirroring, this component refers to the ability to regulate your own feelings. Failure to do so could prove damaging to individuals.

### HINT BOX

*Self-awareness and emotion regulation are especially important for people working in social care, where professional boundaries and relationships are often challenged. Over-identification with the people they take care of, or lack of boundaries, could easily overwhelm these individuals and cause them to burn out.*

## Empathy in practice

Can empathy skills be taught? Can you learn how to develop an empathic capacity that engenders trust and builds bonds? People are born with general emotional intelligence that determines their potential for learning emotional competencies. Research shows that if EQ competencies can be improved, then they are sustainable over a long period of time. Actually, older people show higher levels of empathy, suggesting that empathy may be learned through life experience. The more situations you experience, the easier it will be for you to empathize with others and 'put yourself in their shoes'. So while IQ is very much fixed, EQ can be improved with the right motivation. Below are some hints on how to do this.

## Five steps to improve your empathy skills

1.  Take time to recognize other people's emotions – Empathy is about caring, about sharing other people's feelings. You have to analyse their verbal cues, their body language, read between the lines: What is the person feeling? What do their words mean? This ability can help salespeople understand their customers' needs and create a bond of trust between them; it can also help managers relate better to their staff and understand the factors that trigger their motivation.

2.  See through the eyes of others – Now that you know what others are feeling, you need to place yourself 'in their shoes'. In order to do this, you could imagine yourself in the other person's position and think how you might feel if you were them. Let them know that you understand their feelings. If you are a salesperson, manager, doctor, this ability will help

**HINT BOX**

1.  *Ask people questions about their hobbies,*
    *their challenges, their families, their aspirations:*
    *'That is interesting. Can you say more about that?'*
    *'I wasn't aware of that. Could you tell me more?'*
    *'I'm curious about that ... let's discuss this in more*
    *depth.'*
    *'How do you feel about that? What are some of*
    *your concerns?'*

2.  *Pay attention not only to verbal cues but also to*
    *body language.*

3.  *Listen without judging.*
    *Use active listening; double-check the meaning of*
    *what another person is saying by paraphrasing.*
    *Don't interrupt. Don't change the subject.*
    *Be fully present with body and mind. Don't read*
    *emails, take calls or think of something else.*
    *Encourage people to speak, especially the quiet*
    *ones.*

create the connection and the foundation of trust that will eventually lead to higher sales and/or productivity.

3.  Think before you act – Understanding your own emotions and managing them is very important in leading others and potentially changing minds. This ability is especially important for highly emotional events. In order to deal

with this type of event, you have to pause and think before responding. Think of the reaction triggered by your response, will it lead to the desired results or not? Responding too quickly might also trigger the impression that you do not empathize with the other person. You need also to take into account your non-verbal response; spend some time thinking about how you come across.

4.  Use emotions to drive action – Now that you are in the other person's shoes, you need to help them take a decision. For example, when managing change in the workplace, leaders are advised to use the sense of urgency in order to drive their teams to take actions. Provide the other person with an appropriate vision, communicate with them with empathy, and use these negative or positive feelings to make the changes required.

5.  Use empathy to sell – Empathic skills are extremely useful in developing major sales. Many companies have found that the best people at selling lower value products and services under £5,000 cannot achieve the same success when engaging in major sales above £5,000 and up to millions of pounds. The reason is that the presentation and promotion of the benefits of a particular product may be effective in selling a simple item – such as a watch, for example – because the client's thought processes for a lower cost product are not overly complex. However, when selling a higher priced product (such as property) or service (such as consultancy), the buyer will consider their needs far more carefully.

In developing a major sell, you should not present the benefits of a solution before you have been fully briefed on the client's need. This is because from the client's perspective you cannot solve their problem until you fully understand it, and presenting a solution before this stage will be met with objections. Contrary to popular opinion, sales is not about 'objection handling' but instead about not provoking any objections in the first place.

To understand a business need is a sophisticated skill that you can develop over time. It involves holding meetings with clients and asking open questions, such as 'What are your aspirations for your business?', 'How does this issue affect your business?' or 'How could solving this issue help your business?'. Having empathy and being able to 'see through the eyes of the other' will enable you to really understand your client's needs.

# Case study:
# Anita Roddick's empathy

Anita Roddick, the founder of The Body Shop, was one of the most successful people in the cosmetics industry and the UK's best-known female entrepreneur. As a strong ecologist and feminist, she revolutionized the way cosmetics are sold. Her empathic skills were the source of her success, helping her to understand the feelings of her customers, which in turn enabled her to create The Body Shop as a way of giving women what they had been looking for in cosmetics: pure products not tested on animals. Furthermore, the empathic skills she manifested towards her employees and the 'outside world', created a values-based corporate identity. The Body Shop has a reputation for supporting social and environmental causes thanks to Roddick's strong personal sense of social responsibility. In *Strategic Management*, written in 2006 by Charles Hill and Gareth Jones, Roddick said she believed that 'business should do more than make money, create decent jobs, or sell good products. Rather, business should help solve major social problems such as homelessness, unemployment, and social alienation.'

## Early success

Roddick was born in 1942 in Littlehampton, England, to an immigrant family with four children. She grew up working at her parents' café and originally wanted to become a teacher. After her studies, however, she held several jobs and saved money in order to go travelling.

In 1976 Roddick founded The Body Shop, creating cosmetics containing ingredients that women used in traditional cleansing rituals, rituals she had witnessed while on her travels. Part of the secret of The Body Shop's early success was that it had its own unique market niche. At a time when the cosmetics industry was making exaggerated claims about scientific advancements in skin care, Roddick was able to understand some women's need for natural products.

## Ethical selling

The Body Shop was the first company to prohibit testing on animals and one of the first to encourage fair trade in Third World countries. Her products especially appealed to upscale, mainly middle-class women who saw The Body Shop as an ethical alternative to the beauty-at-any-price stance of the more fashion-driven cosmetics companies. But it was also an emotional appeal, one that promised customers that by buying its products they were also doing something good for the planet.

In 1984 the company went public and spread franchises all over England. Four years later, in 1988, the first Body Shop store was opened in New York City. By 1997, the company boasted 1,500 stores, including franchises, in forty-seven countries.

## Emotional bonds

By the mid-1990s, however, The Body Shop faced growing competition, so the company began its first major advertising initiative. The campaign figured Ruby, a doll of Rubenesque proportions, and had a blunt message on the campaign poster: 'There are 3 billion women who don't look like supermodels and only 8 who do.' The campaign not only questioned the ideal of an exceptionally thin body, but also promoted a nude 'size 18' doll as an example of beauty. Through this campaign, the company positioned itself against an idea that had long dominated the fashion industry, that there was an ideal beauty to which all women should aspire. Ruby was followed by two more issues-oriented campaigns that focused on domestic violence and ageing. Again, Roddick's empathic skills allowed the company to create an emotional bond with its customers, the company receiving thousands of calls and letters of appreciation for Ruby's realistic portrayal of beauty. 'It makes you feel better about yourself', one of the customers said. In an interview regarding the Ruby campaign, Roddick talked about Ruby's creation:

The girls in [British fashion magazines] are exactly what the media wants … they have no bodies, they're too thin. They are passive. They are, you know, beaten up. So, we – three of us in my office – we came up with this broadsheet which was called 'Full Voice'. It was like a pamphlet on the body and self-esteem … As the personification of The Body Shop's commitment to self-esteem, Ruby is more than just an image; she's a state of mind – strong, independent and informed. She doesn't weigh her self-esteem against false standards. She loves her body and is true to herself.

In 2006, The Body Shop became an independently managed subsidiary of the L'Oréal Group. In 2008, it had over 2,500 stores in fifty-five different markets. Its success put Roddick's net worth at more than $200 million.

 ## What you have learned about empathy

In this chapter you have seen that understanding other people through empathy skills is crucial to selling yourself. Not only will empathy boost your career prospects and help you achieve your goals, but it will also improve your relationships. We saw in the case of The Body Shop how empathy skills can help business people create bonds of trust and confidence with their clients, which then enable them to communicate with their market on every level.

# Step 6:
# Under-Promise and Over-Deliver

'My approach is a simple one:
Promise less, deliver more.'
**Michael Howard**

## Why under-promise and over-deliver?

As important as image and appearance can be in business, you will ultimately be evaluated on the quality of your work. This means keeping to every promise you make, carefully understanding what is expected of you, and delivering more. There are no short cuts, and this involves hard work and professionalism to ensure you do every job to the best of your ability and positively exceed people's expectations.

### Maintain honesty and integrity

Making promises you cannot keep will mean that others will lose faith in you and ultimately stop doing business with you. People have antennae for manipulation and will notice any half-truths or lies you tell. Sincerity, on the other hand, is much more powerful and people will detect if you genuinely believe what you say.

Business is a long journey and you will need to develop and maintain relationships. Under-promising and over-delivering will help you come across as trustworthy and sincere, and will provide true benefits such as:

- Enhanced trust
- Long-term relationships
- Repeat business.

## How this chapter will help you to under-promise and over-deliver

*Learn how to complete a project with excellence:*

- *Assess properly the work needed to complete a task, and understand what you should communicate to your boss (under-promise):*
  1. *Agree deliverables*
  2. *Be MECE (see page 102)*

- *Gain efficiency that will enable you to deliver before a set deadline and better (over-deliver):*
  1. *Design the working plan*
  2. *Always prioritize (the 80/20 rule)*
  3. *Anticipate the next steps*

- *Learn how to raise the right level of expectation, and play carefully with the balance between under-promising and over-delivering:*
  1. *Manage your boss's expectations*
  2. *No matter if you under or over-promise, never under-deliver*

# How to complete a project with excellence

Tom Peter's formula for success, first written in the *Chicago Tribune*, has become a famous business tip. Behind the maxim 'under-promise, over-deliver' lies the problem of a raised expectation. Each time someone asks you to complete a project (whether a study, a recommendation or a simple presentation), this work raises expectations on their part. It is necessary for you to be able to manage their expectations, not only for this piece of work but also for any others that follow.

## Agreeing deliverables

The ability to quickly assess the amount of work to be delivered is a great skill. Many people tend to over-promise to their boss because they make a mistake when assessing the amount of work to be completed. When you communicate on the project delivery, you should agree on two points: the deliverables and the timeline.

First of all, make sure that you agree on the deliverables. It may be clearly stated, for example: 'I want a ten-slides PowerPoint presentation on the sales of the past month.' In this case, the deliverables are clear and you can start to assess the work to be done.

But in other instances the deliverables may be vague or too general, for example: 'I want an assessment of opportunities to expand our business into another European country.' In this case, you need to ask for more details about what is expected of you: 'Do you mean all of Europe or only the biggest national markets?'; 'What do you mean by expanding into a market?'; 'Do you want a Word document, or a PowerPoint presentation?'. Once you agree on the deliverables, you will then need to assess the work to be done.

## Assessing a workload

There is a very simple method of assessing the amount of work required. The key is to break down the deliverables into small and quantifiable actions so that you can build your project plan.

Start by taking a look at the deliverables and decide how to best break them into 'sub-deliverables'. For example, if one of the deliverables is a feasibility assessment on the market penetration of France and Germany, you will create a list for both markets regarding the possibilities of your company entering each market. Be careful when listing the options and make sure you use MECE (see below) when breaking down your points.

## MECE

What is MECE? When you analyse, you need to be logical and coherent, and you need to avoid becoming confused. A method used by the best management consultants to analyse a project logically is MECE – Mutually Exclusive and Collectively Exhaustive.

Firstly, this involves finding a way of listing all aspects in a project so that they do not overlap (mutually exclusive), and ensuring that the aggregated list covers all possibilities (collectively exhaustive). In our case, you could come up with the following list:

- Sell from the UK

- Start operations in France and Germany

- Hire a sales agent

- Sign an agreement with a local distributor

- Create a joint venture

- Buy a local company.

Secondly, try to break down the options even further by actions to be taken to assess the work properly. For example: 'How do I assess the feasibility option of signing an agreement with local distributors?' To achieve MECE, follow a step-by-step process:

- Do a market screening of the distributors

- See which competitors are already in contact with them

- Contact the most relevant ones

- Understand If they would be interested in distributing your product.

It is now very easy for you to assess the amount of work needed to assess this option. You can even put a time at the end of each action:

- Do a market screening of the distributors (three days)

- See which competitors are already in contact with them (one day)

- Contact the most relevant ones (one day)

- Understand if they would be interested in distributing your product (seven days).

Thirdly, if you do the same for each action and sum the time of all actions, you will come up with a timescale. Now pay attention, this is NOT the deadline you should communicate to your boss or client. It is important that you understand which actions you fully control or that only you can influence. For example, the market screening of distributors will not take more than three days, but contacting the most relevant distributors for your business may take more than one day. You don't know how easy it will be to reach the good contacts in the organization, or how fast they will respond to you. For those actions you do not fully control, you can raise the time allotted by 50 per cent to get to a fair assumption of the time needed.

Fourthly, you need to understand whether you want to under-promise and how to communicate it to your boss or client. When you communicate a deadline on the delivery of an agreed end product, you raise an expectation. You cannot move this deadline afterwards. You may have good reasons (e.g., 'I put a lot of effort in identifying the key contacts among the distributors but they haven't responded'), but this is not your boss's or client's problem. Remember what the poet Robert W. Service said: 'A promise made is a debt unpaid.' If you are afraid of not being able to deliver on time, do not hesitate to add 20 per cent more time on the deadline before communicating it. However, be careful not to overly extend the deadline, as it would mean lowering your boss's expectations – which could be a huge handicap if you are an ambitious person willing to grow fast in a company.

## How to over-achieve

Once you have agreed on the end products and the deadline, you need to deliver faster and better. There are a number of things you can do to gain efficiency in your work and be able to over-achieve, making your boss or client happy.

When you start the project the first thing to do is to take your project plan and see where you can improve the process. Returning to our example, if you need to assess the opportunities to enter the European market in ten days, you should take your project plan and see which action points you could shrink so that you deliver in eight days instead. Once you have identified them, see how you can complete those actions more swiftly.

## Pareto rule

There is an important tip that you should always keep in mind: the 80/20 rule. This principle was created by the Italian economist Vilfredo Pareto in 1906 when he discovered that 20 per cent of the population in Italy owned 80 per cent of the land, the same way that 20 per cent of the pea pods in his garden contained 80 per cent of the peas. The 80/20 rule, also called the law of the vital few, states that in many cases, 80 per cent of the effects come from 20 per cent of the causes. It is quite likely that this rule applies to your industry too, so do not waste time, focus on the key elements. For example, in the pharmaceutical industry 20 per cent of the European countries represent 80 per cent of the EU market (Germany, France, UK, Spain and Italy). You should then concentrate on these markets, as the rest are less significant.

Getting back to our task, you said that you would do a market screening of the distributors in three days? We suggest you do it in two days, focusing on the 20 per cent of the distributors who make the 80 per cent of the business!

## Quick wins

Another useful approach is to focus on the Quick Wins. Before starting any analysis, try to begin with the easiest options. For example, if there is a distributor you have identified in the key 20 per cent and you have some reliable information on this distributor, then begin with this one. Starting with the Quick Wins is key, especially if you are asked for an update in which case you can demonstrate that you are making great progress.

## Next steps

Last but not least, you should always try to anticipate the next steps in order to over-deliver. Think about what your boss or client will ask you next. If you are one step ahead, you can start sketching new studies and preparing another presentation. The more creative you are the better. Your boss will always be happy to see that you are producing more than he/she asks. Anticipating the next steps is a great way to over-achieve.

## Managing expectations

This section of the chapter is very important in making sure that you fully exploit the 'under-promise, over-deliver' rule. As we said before, each time you are asked to do one thing, there is also something else expected in return. The graph below describes the feeling of your client at the time of project delivery, depending on what expectations you raised and what your end product is.

- If you set low expectations (you under-promised) and you under-deliver, you will be ignored. Your client or boss will not even consider your work.

- If you set high expectations (you over-promised) and you under-deliver, your client will be angry. This is the worst-case scenario as your client is expecting a lot from you and you are not able to achieve what you made a commitment to do.

- If you set too low expectations (you under-promised too much) and over-deliver, your client will be bored. You over-achieved but somehow he/she knew that you could do better and is not particularly surprised that you over-delivered.

- If you set high expectations (you over-promised) and you over-deliver, your boss will be delighted.

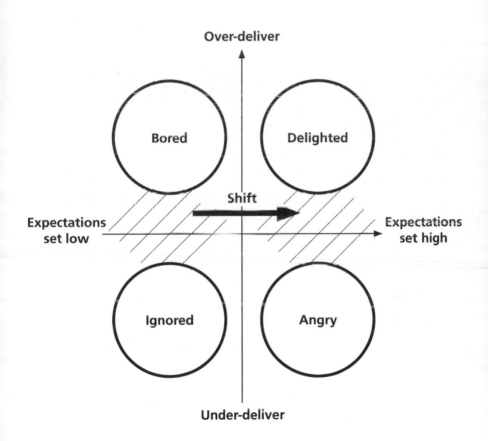

## Dealing with changing expectations

You need to take into consideration the fact that as you over-deliver, there is a shift of expectations from your boss or client. If you over-deliver several times in a row, there are two possible explanations.

- The first is that you are very good, and this raises their expectations for the upcoming projects.

- The second is that you are average but you under-promise, in which case each time you try to under-promise they will expect more from you.

In both cases there is a shift in expectation. That is why it is important that you always over-deliver, but you should alternate between setting high and low expectations. To reduce the shift in expectations, it is a good idea to make your boss or client feel a little bored some of the time.

# Case study: The Google IPO

In 2004, Google's announcement that it was ready for an Initial Public Offer (IPO) drew substantial attention. An IPO is the first sale of stock by a company to the public enabling ordinary people to buy shares and in many cases the founders to generate significant wealth. Google had been founded in 1998 by two Stanford University PhD students, Sergey Brin and Larry Page, going on to become one of the most successful companies on the Internet.

Brin and Page developed Google based on a simple lesson they drew from academia. They realized that the footnotes in academic texts provide a useful way of recognizing popular and relevant books. Put simply, the more references a book received in footnotes, the more important that book was. They applied the same principle to the Internet; they created a search engine that ranked web pages – by using links to other websites – in order to rank their relevance.

They had found a way of searching the Internet that became so popular among users all around the world that the verb 'Googled' entered the *Oxford English Dictionary* in 2006.

## Under-promising

However, the company had been fairly quiet about how popular they had become or how much money they were making. Its core business was selling search-based advertising (companies would purchase key words that users entered on Internet searches). The benefit for the advertiser was that potential customers with direct interest in their type of product or service would come to them. This turns the traditional advertising model on its head, where there is a shotgun approach in which you advertise to many people who aren't the real targets in the hope of finding the ones who are interested in you.

Google had not wanted its competitors to know how effectively this advertising system was working both for the company itself and its customers. It had 'under-promised' to the market by not fully exploiting the attention and credibility it could have gained by talking about its sales.

## Over-delivering

In 2004, in the filing for its IPO, Google 'over-delivered' by announcing that the company had been very profitable since 2001. Google had generated revenues of $961.9 million in 2003, with a net profit of $106.5 million. Sales had increased 177 per cent from the year before, and for the first quarter of 2004, Google had sales of $389.6 million, with a net income of $64 million, up 148 per cent from the first quarter of 2003.

In 2004 the Google founders emphasized this message of honesty, of over-delivering rather than under-delivering on their promises:

> In Warren Buffett's words, 'We won't "smooth" quarterly or annual results: If earnings figures are lumpy when they reach headquarters, they will be lumpy when they reach you.'

The IPO was not without controversy as Page and Brin gave an unorthodox interview to *Playboy* magazine during the 'quiet period' (in which companies should not release further information), which led to an investigation by the US Securities and Exchange Commission. Google under-promised again by lowering the share price to $85 per share and it also lowered the number of shares being sold by company executives. The changes reduced the value of Google substantially.

## Record-breaking

Google eventually offered 19,605,052 shares at $85 per share; the price was the same for everyone. The IPO raised $1.67 billion, setting the market capitalization to a record-breaking $23 billion. The Google IPO was a success and on the day of the introduction, CNNmoney.com reported that the share price had risen by 18 per cent. The 'money left on the table' was limited and the company had clearly under-promised in setting the pricing at $85 per share. Both founders became instant billionaires. But the company clearly over-delivered to the initial investors; according to Internetnews. com, Yahoo, for example, was issued 2.7 million of shares with a total value of $229 million. By February 2011, Google stock was being traded at $610 per share, more than 700 per cent the price of the initial share – meaning that, up until today, Google has over-delivered many times over to those who trusted it with their money.

## 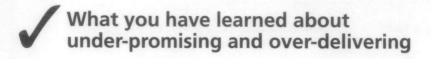 What you have learned about under-promising and over-delivering

In this chapter you have learned the importance of keeping to your word in order to sell yourself. This involves first managing and then exceeding expectations by over-delivering on what you promise. You have also learned how to work on your project management skills, so that you can assess what you are being asked and execute what is required of you. This will enable you to maintain honesty and integrity, build trust with your boss and/or clients, and develop prosperous long-term work relationships.

# Step 7:
# Going the Extra Mile

'Be a yardstick of quality. Some people aren't used to an environment where excellence is expected.'
**Steve Jobs**

## Why is going the extra mile important?

Doing a job to the expected standard is what you are paid to do. But it will not enable you to impress others and accelerate quickly through your career. In order to sell yourself to others, add real value and climb the corporate ladder, you will need to go the extra mile.

Going the extra mile is a mental attitude and you have to make this attitude your personal trademark. It is a way of thinking you need to develop in order to have success in everything that you do. This chapter is divided in two sections: Section 1 will help you to develop a mindset that allows you to go the extra mile, while Section 2 will show you how to execute your goals.

# How this chapter will help you go the extra mile

*Learn important things about going the extra mile, including how to:*

- *Produce your mental shift*
- *Focus on the widely important*
- *Challenge with candour*

*Learn to focus on the widely important goals and go the extra mile in your life:*

- *Lead measures and key actions*
- *Develop a scoreboard and track your success*
- *Build a planning and accounting system to get all your work done*

## Section 1: Produce your mental shift

On 5 November 2009, Steve Jobs was ranked as the CEO of the decade by *Fortune* magazine. Co-founder of Apple and Pixar (now part of Disney), he helped invent the PC as we know it and changed the way people use technology, with such products as the Mac, iPhone and the iPad.

What made him go the extra mile? There are certain key personal traits possessed by Mr Jobs which everyone can develop: the search for perfection, inspiration, continuous improvement and, oh yes, making money.

## Strive for perfection

Going the extra mile is about performing at the highest level in everything you do. Every time you perform a task you have to be truly obsessed about the quality of what you deliver. In some cases it will not be quite possible to achieve the quality you managed in the past, but remember it is the attitude that counts.

Steve Jobs is commonly known as a perfectionist. Sometimes this means working overnight and weekends, and unfortunately not seeing his family for a while. Jobs rehearses for hours before each presentation and he threw away numerous iPod designs just before its launch in 2001 because he knew they were not quite right. Going the extra mile means taking care so that the final outcome is perfect.

## Think different and take the initiative

'Think different' is an advertising slogan created by Apple Computer Inc. in 1997. It is not easy to think out of the box, but it is worth trying. Apple based its own success on innovative technology, and this was possible just because they used to think different. In everyday life, there are so many occasions for identifying new ideas that it is worth trying. Taking the initiative means improving the way you work and starting something without have to be asked. Think different by trying to offer your manager or your family something new and unexpected.

## Challenge with candour to produce a cultural shift

Another esteemed business leader, Jack Welch (see Step 10), one of the most successful business people in history, says that 'Candour in business – or in any kind of organization – is a rare and wondrous thing'. What he basically means is that having a candid attitude towards every subject and applying it to any conversation ultimately leads to improvement. Challenging with candour should first start from a personal perspective: challenge yourself to improve your own understanding of your job and the people around you, and ultimately try to understand yourself better. Every time things are not clear, try to ask yourself 'the reason why' and look for the answer. This will enable you to produce a mental shift.

## Be interesting

Ok, you did a great job, but sometimes it is just not enough. People can be so busy that sometimes it is not easy to get noticed. Therefore, you need to make your efforts interesting. Be ready to use every opportunity to do so. Arrive early at the office, leave after your manager, and why are you not cooking something special for your family this Sunday?

## Making money

The law of compensation states that everything you do will come back amplified to you in the future. Therefore, every time you want to benefit from this law you have to give in the first place, without worrying about the immediate outcome of your actions.

Find a metric to measure how your efforts are reimbursed. It may be the preference of your customers, the consideration of your friends, or even your salary. Give more in the first place and be ready to see the results.

In an interview with Peter Burrows in *Bloomberg Businessweek* in 2004, Steve Jobs declared: 'We [Apple] do things where we feel we can make a significant contribution. That's one of my other beliefs.' This means that every time he sells a product, he wants to make a profit. It may sound counter-intuitive, but many companies accept to make some loss in order to increase their position in the marketplace. Going the extra mile consists of creating something so unique and high quality that everybody will recognize it and be glad to pay for it, making you more money.

# Section 2: Execution

The world is notoriously full of people with good intentions. Some of them succeed, some don't. In this Section, you will learn how to maximize your chance of success and the first step is to clearly define your goals. There are just a few things that really matter in goal setting: be realistic and audacious, and remember to focus on the widely important.

## Be audacious

In Step 1 you developed your target. Now you can take that target further to develop an audacious goal. All of us have a dream and you have a dream for yourself. Can you imagine yourself in five years' time? Concentrate a few seconds on what you really want. Let this exercise drive your imagination. Done it? Unless you see yourself as the future Prime Minister, think again and try a little harder: think about the objective you want to achieve and imagine success. Imagine how you will feel in that moment and how you will behave. Use your mind as a positive driver and believe in yourself: that will be your audacious goal. Now use that vision to create a realistic but audacious three-year goal:

My three key values

1)_____

2)_____

3)_____

My three key features

1)_____

2)_____

3)_____

My three-year audacious goal:

_____


Why is this goal so important to me?

_____

## Focus on the widely important

Once you set your goal, comes the interesting part: make your objective become true. If you look around, you may realize that many people fail miserably as they try to fulfil their goals. People sometimes feel so overwhelmed by their daily routine that they can get paralysed and lose focus on what really matters ... on the widely important. What are the main steps for your success? Prioritization is the key.

Every time you plan something, define clearly your goal and remember to write a list of the key activities that need to be implemented.

Do you want to become a Senior Manager? You will probably need management training. Are you planning to enter a business school? You probably need to set some criteria in order to select the right one. You will have to check what the latest rankings are and if there are scholarship schemes, for example. Maybe you need to meet some academic requirements or take a test like the GMAT (Graduate Management Admission Test). There are a number of aspects to consider. So prioritize.

Come back to your audacious three-year goal and list the key activities you need to undertake in order to get started. Think of them in terms of importance and put them in order.

Key activities

1)_____

2)_____

3)_____

## Make propositions actionable

Have you noticed? Some propositions are likely to be executed in a straightforward way, some others not. What is the fundamental difference between them? In many cases, it simply depends on the ability to put the proposition into action. Proposed solution: start by defining a concrete desired goal and then work backwards. In this way you can map every step of the process into actions and clarify each intermediate goal you want to achieve. Remember that every step needs to be actionable, with clear results and objectives. Consider again the activities you need to perform to achieve your goal, and make them actionable.

> ### Example:
> Goal: *Train for London marathon*.
> Not actionable proposition: *I will start to look for a gym*.
> Actionable proposition: *I am going to the gym and I will schedule my activities with a trainer.*

Key **actionable** activities

1)_____

2)_____

3)_____

## Divide and conquer

Now that you have created a list of actionable activities, break them into parts; these will be the micro-activities that need to be executed. Macro-activities will be your milestones, and you will always tend to them while performing your micro-activities.

Actionable milestones and activities

1)_____

- _____

- _____

- _____

2)_____

- _____

- _____

- _____

3)_____

- _____

- _____

- _____

## Set your deadlines

Once you have your detailed list, start to assign deadlines to each of
your activities. Having a time constraint will force you to be tight to
your activities. Please, follow your time intentions once you set them.

Actionable milestones and activities          Deadline

1)_____          _____

   • _____          _____

   • _____          _____

   • _____          _____

2)_____          _____

   • _____          _____

   • _____          _____

   • _____          _____

3)_____          _____

   • _____          _____

   • _____          _____

   • _____          _____

## Lead measures

Measuring is such an important activity that it should become your obsession. You need to identify some metrics to measure your activities and to understand how close you are to your goal.

> ### Example of the marathon:
> **Actionable proposition:** *I am going to the gym and I will schedule my activities with a trainer.*
> - *Number of times per week at the gym.*
> - *Number of miles per week.*

## Over-achieve

Keep yourself hungry every day. You have to strive for delivering more results and value, and this is something you do for yourself. To have success you need to be firm and committed. Try to surprise yourself over achieving your objective, increasing the expectation on your lead measures.

## Learn lessons

Whatever happens, at the end of each activity, remember to practise reviewing the 'lessons learned' from any of your initiatives. Try to look at all the propositions in a rational way. Explain to a friend what actions you undertook, and clearly underline your success and the weaknesses of the process. Be candid. What went well? Where did you fall short? What processes could have been better? Did you meet your time commitments? If not, why? Use this information to improve processes and hold yourself accountable.

Your personal scoreboard:

Actionable milestones and activities                    Deadline

1)_____          _____

   • _____          _____

   • _____          _____

   • _____          _____

2)_____          _____

   • _____          _____

   • _____          _____

   • _____          _____

3)_____          _____

   • _____          _____

   • _____          _____

   • _____          _____

## Reward yourself

The person you are going to share most of your life with is yourself. Have you thought about that? Then learn to reward your own success when you get things done. This will keep motivation high. You know

| Lead Measures | Strengths/ Weaknesses | Lessons Learnt |
|---|---|---|
| _____ | _____ | _____ |
| _____ | _____ | _____ |
| _____ | _____ | _____ |
| _____ | _____ | _____ |
| _____ | _____ | _____ |
| _____ | _____ | _____ |
| _____ | _____ | _____ |
| _____ | _____ | _____ |
| _____ | _____ | _____ |
| _____ | _____ | _____ |
| _____ | _____ | _____ |
| _____ | _____ | _____ |

how to do it. It can be a small weekend break, a concert, a book or just a beer with your friends. Congratulate yourself for every achievement.

# Case study:
# Jeff Bezos and getting bigger faster

The benefits of going the extra mile in business are perfectly demonstrated by Jeff Bezos, the founder of Amazon.com. Bezos's business philosophy of going the extra mile is summed up by his motto 'get, big, fast'.

In 1994, at the age of thirty, Jeff Bezos was the Senior Vice President of D.E. Shaw in New York. The firm specialized in the application of computer science to the stock market and provided Bezos with a stable career and a very high salary (reputed to be $1 million a year).

One day, Bezos, a computer science and electrical engineering graduate from Princeton, noticed that Internet usage was increasing at 2,300 per cent each year. This incredible rate of growth led Bezos to assess the best opportunities for an Internet business. At that time, he noted that mail order companies did not generally focus on books (as an inventory list of all the available books would be too large to post). The book market was enormous with over 500 million books expected to be ordered that year, but without any one company dominating market share. Bezos's idea was for an Internet site with a large database to list all the books and supply the market twenty-four hours a day anywhere in the world.

## Seize the opportunity

Bezos was faced with a clear business opportunity, but he had to leave a secure job with excellent earning potential. Should he risk these strong career prospects? Was it not better to settle for what he already had rather than going the extra mile to create a new type of business?

Bezos took the leap, gave up his job and began setting up the website Amazon, named after the largest river in the world. Uniquely, he named the company Amazon.com. Today, it is common to talk about dot-coms, but Amazon was the first and it differentiated the business.

Bezos helped with the original Internet set-up himself through his knowledge of computer science. In 1995, Amazon. com went live and – without the support of a marketing budget – was soon selling books across the United States.

One of the secrets of Amazon.com's success was price. Normal bookstores need to have buildings, sales people, phones, insurance, advertising, etc. Amazon.com was able to reduce all these overheads with just a small warehouse, offering instead an online platform facilitating sales of tens of thousands of books to millions of customers.

Amazon.com also had software that kept track of what customers were buying and then recommended similar books to them. Bezos focused on improving customer service; Amazon became known as one of the most secure places from which to buy products on the Internet. The business began to grow at a startling rate and after two years it was ready to go public.

## Going the extra mile

Bezos's own family had invested in Amazon.com and by the end of the 1990s he and his parents were collectively worth hundreds of millions of dollars. Bezos had achieved in a few years what most people do not manage in a lifetime. Was it time to give up the business and reflect on his achievements? Perhaps he should cash in on his stake and live a life of luxury? Maybe Amazon was just a flash-in-the-pan success and would crash with the dot-com bubble?

In 2002, Bezos again went the extra mile. He changed Amazon. com from a bookstore to an online retailer for many other products, such as electronics, computers, toys, music and clothing. He even launched a search engine and an online sports retailer. Amazon. com also launched a number of innovative services – such as the Advantage for Music programme which enabled independent musicians to sell their music to online buyers.

By 2005, Amazon.com had sales over $10 billion. Bezos again saw an opportunity to go the extra mile and he launched the 'Kindle', an electronic reading machine. Rather than purchasing physical books through Amazon.com, customers can now buy lower cost e-books that are instantly downloadable on their Kindles. The sales of Kindles reached over $2 billion in 2010, increasing 200 per cent per year. In May 2011, Amazon announced that it is now selling more e-book units for its Kindle device than hardback and paperback books combined.

Today, Amazon.com is the largest online retailer in the United States with sales over $20 billion and over 30,000 employees. Jeff Bezos's remarkable ascent shows how going the extra mile can take you on a stratospheric rise to the top.

# ✔ What you have learned about going the extra mile

In this chapter, you have learned how to develop a mental attitude that will help you go the extra mile. You have also developed a scoreboard to help you execute your goals. You started from the goal definition and progressed to the list of all the actionable activities you need to implement. Then you created a set of lead measures and deadlines to monitor your progress. You have learned how to keep track of your strengths and weaknesses, and – most of all – you learned that every single process has at least one lesson to be learned.

# Step 8:
# Overcoming Setbacks

'There is no education like adversity.'
**Benjamin Disraeli**

## Why is overcoming setbacks important?

Sadly, it is quite certain that you will fail or face a setback in a particular aspect of business. Human beings make mistakes and business is unpredictable. The result is that most business people continuously deal with adversity and failure. The list of prominent people who have actually reached rock bottom and filed for bankruptcy includes some of those listed as celebrated business gurus, such as Donald Trump, Henry Ford and Walt Disney.

# How this chapter will help you to overcome setbacks

*Learn important things about overcoming setbacks, including:*

- *Bounce Back*
- *Expect the unexpected*
- *Develop a setback pipeline*
- *Put things in perspective*
- *Turn the situation to your advantage*
- *Learn from mistakes*
- *Create a plan of action*
- *Change what you do, not what you are about*
- *Persevere*

# So, who suffers setbacks?

## Companies fail

At the company level, failure, adversity and setback are widespread. For example, in the US, in 2001, 257 companies with $258 billion in assets declared bankruptcy. Also in this period, twenty-six of the largest US firms saw two-thirds of their market value drop – including HP, Cisco and AOL Time Warner. In September 2008 the $600 billion investment bank Lehman Brothers collapsed almost overnight, and became the largest bankruptcy in world history.

## Nations suffer

The same adversity is even common at the national level. In 2010, these OECD countries registered national deficits: United States −10.7 per cent; Japan −8.2 per cent; Germany 5.3 per cent; France 8.6 per cent; Italy 5.4 per cent; United Kingdom 13.3 per cent (figures are as a percentage of GDP). Greece was so close to financial ruin in 2010 that it had to receive a bailout package from the EU/IMF for $61 billion. At the time of writing, Greece, Portugal and Spain have a 'credibility problem', simply because they lack the ability to adequately repay high deficits due to a low growth rate.

## Economies go bust

In the late 1990s, Gordon Brown, the British Chancellor of the Exchequer, announced the end of the 'boom and bust' economic cycle, only to end his term as Prime Minister a decade later following the worst financial crisis in seventy years and an economic recession. The simple reality is that no matter what policy politicians have implemented, there has remained an economic cycle that includes positive growth, but also negative contraction.

# How do you overcome setbacks?

## Bounce back

Whether a businessman, a company or a nation, a key differentiator of success is not the absence of failure or adversity, but the ability to bounce back and try again. Indeed, many studies have attempted to uncover the common qualities of prosperous entrepreneurs but found them to be a highly disparate bunch with only one shared trait: perseverance.

## Expect the unexpected

Nassim Nicholas Taleb described in his book *The Black Swan* how the absolutely unpredictable and unexpected has been a key determinant of change in our world. The term 'Black Swan' refers to the presumption in the Middle Ages that all swans were white – this was because every reported swan up to that time had been white. Then, in 1697, Dutch explorer Willem De Vlamingh discovered black swans and the definition of a swan was changed for ever. Taleb uses this analogy to show how even things perceived to be impossible still regularly happen. In the same way, Malcolm Gladwell in his book *The Tipping Point* showed that there have been turning points that have created new economic landscapes. Gladwell uses tipping points in the world to explain, for example, the sudden decline in crime in New York City, or the worldwide commercial take-off of fashion items such as Hush Puppies shoes. The fundamental point is that there will be unexpected, unpredicted major events, such as those seen on 11 September 2001.

## Develop a setback pipeline

Being prepared for failure is a mental attitude you should acquire. In each forecast you make, you should have an optimistic, a moderate and a pessimistic scenario. This enables you to prepare in advance for unfavourable outcomes. You can also develop a setback pipeline. For example, I estimate that I will have a 1 in 10 chance of success at a job interview. Therefore, it will require ten interviews before I receive a job offer, so I have to ensure I achieve this number of interviews.

## Put things in perspective

There will be times when your business goes worse than even your most pessimistic forecast. When facing real setbacks, you need to keep things in perspective. Perhaps your business has gone terribly, horrendously even, but there are many people in far worse situations. The world is full of disadvantaged people who with great courage and bravery overcome adversity against the most daunting odds. For example, Jean-Dominique Bauby was a successful professional and the Editor of the French *Elle* magazine. He unexpectedly suffered a massive stroke that rendered him paralysed and immobile, except for the movement of his left eye. His mind was not damaged, and incredibly he managed to develop a means of communications by organizing the letters of the alphabet by their frequency. When a letter was read out loud which matched the letter in the word he was thinking, he would blink. Brilliantly, he used this method to write his memoirs, which became a best-selling book (*The Diving Bell and the Butterfly*) and then a successful film. Jean-Dominique Bauby exemplifies how people do suffer great setbacks but they can also bounce back to achieve amazing feats.

## Turn the situation to your advantage

As well as planning for damaging effects to your business, you should also look for emergent business opportunities. Change can mean both good and bad for your business. Following each setback, you should actively consider if there is any way you can turn what happened to your advantage.

## Learn from mistakes

Even though failure happens to everyone, it does happen for a reason. You need to learn from every mistake. Business is constantly changing and there is no predetermined formula; rather, it is a process of trial and error. It is a matter of continuously learning what didn't work at the time and what will work in future. This education forms your experience and enables you to be successful in the future.

## Create a plan of action

Write down your challenges and analyse what has gone wrong and how you can solve the situation. For example, a businessman we know, who ran a high-quality and well-known design agency in London, went bankrupt in 2010. He reassessed his business and realized that while he was generating a lot of business as the MD, he couldn't sustain the fixed costs of the company (such as office rent and full-time employees). He therefore decided to relaunch his business as just himself, utilizing his staff on a freelance basis, as and when they were required. His company is now more profitable than it has ever been.

To create a plan of action, ask yourself:

- What is your true core business? What creates the cash?
- Are you overextending yourself? Have you invested too much in growth?
- Have you been measuring performance effectively? Have you been letting go of underachievers?
- Have you been keeping true to your strategy?

## Change what you do, not what you are about

The point is to change how you have been doing business, not change yourself as a person. In *Ruthless Execution*, Amir Hartman explores what business leaders at large companies (such as Cisco, GE and IBM) do when their companies 'hit the financial wall'. He defines three key things to do:

- **Recalibrate your strategies** – Think about what you should do. Rearrange your business interests and reassess how your resources are being allocated.

- **Recalibrate your rules** – After knowing what you are going to do, you need to establish new rules that focus on results.

- **Recalibrate your business** – Develop the capabilities you need which will get you to where you want to go.

## Persevere

Sir Richard Branson once accounted for his success in business with the three words 'persevere, persevere, and persevere'. This perfectly illustrates that the difference between successful people and underachievers is the ability to bounce back and try again. Every setback is a learning opportunity, and once you have been through it, you can come back more experienced and with more prospects for success.

# Case study:
# Peter Jones's determination

The British entrepreneur Peter Jones dreamed of being a multimillionaire from childhood. He would climb into the chair behind his father's desk and imagine what it would be like to be a rich businessman in charge of a large company. He showed entrepreneurial flair from a young age, setting up a tennis academy at the age of sixteen. In his early twenties, he had a thriving computer business and the trappings of success with a Porsche and a detached house.

However, Jones overextended himself and didn't manage his cash flow properly. His company went bankrupt and he was forced to move back home with his parents. He was facing failure, and watching his childhood dreams of money and success fade into obscurity.

He later launched a computer support business, followed by a restaurant, but again both of these businesses failed. These setbacks had another effect on Jones though. They gave him a deep determination to improve his situation. He now wanted wealth and success so bad it hurt.

## Bouncing back

At the age of twenty-eight Jones got a job with a large corporate company, Siemens Nixdorf, and channelled his ambitions into work. Within a year, he had become the head of the company's PC business in the UK.

Jones wanted more and was willing to risk everything to get there. In April 2008 he set up his own company Phones International Group with little financing, even sleeping on the office floor at the very beginning. His business grew rapidly, though, and by the turn of the twenty-first century he was generating revenue of £44 million a year.

According to the *Sunday Times Rich List* 2011 Peter Jones is now worth £220 million. His business interests include telecommunications, television, food and the environment, and he employs over 1,000 people. He is also celebrated as a 'Dragon' on the UK television programme *Dragons' Den*, receiving pitches from budding entrepreneurs who want to recreate his success and become multimillionaires themselves.

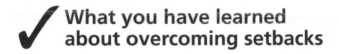

## What you have learned about overcoming setbacks

In this chapter, you have seen that success in business does not rest on simply avoiding problems. Rather, dealing with pitfalls and drawbacks is part of business. How you respond to challenging circumstances will be a key determinant of your success. In order to overcome setbacks, expect the unexpected, keep things in perspective, bounce back and – most importantly – persevere.

# Step 9:
# Managing the Media

'We're building toward a web
where the default is social.'
**Mark Zuckerberg**

## Why manage the media?

In the twenty-first century, the importance of the media for business is greater than ever. With the rise of the Internet, the traditional forms of media – books, television, newspapers and radio – have been joined by new media. The world is more interconnected and it is possible to reach more people than ever before. Information is more readily available than at any other point in history.

Correspondingly, managing the media is even more crucial to selling yourself. Imagine you have developed an innovative product that exactly corresponds to the needs of the market. In this case, you are the product, as a professional with skills and experiences. However, it is not enough to simply acquire these talents. It is equally important to develop an optimal promotion strategy. A carefully developed media strategy can help to develop a solid business reputation, expand your client network and open up career opportunities.

# How this chapter will help you manage the media

*Learn how to manage the media, including:*

*Traditional Media:*

- *Focus on mainstream media*
- *Develop your key messages*
- *Get noticed*
- *Thought leadership*
- *Move on the news agenda*

*New Media:*

- *The importance of new media*
- *Social media*
- *Focus on your target*
- *Unique Selling Points (USPs)*
- *Position yourself*
- *Network*
- *Get your message right*
- *Execute the new media strategy*
- *Analyse, adapt and improve*
- *Be responsible about what you share*

# Section 1: Traditional media

## Focus on mainstream media

The media world has changed a lot in recent years, with the introduction of citizen journalism, blogs and user interest websites. However, the really credible media – of newspapers, television and radio programmes, and trade publications with gravitas – is still the place to be seen and heard.

## Develop your key messages

Before engaging with the mainstream media, plan your objectives. Use your values to develop the key messages that you want to promote to the media.

Write a list of the key messages that you would like to promote:

1. _____

2. _____

3. _____

4. _____

5. _____

7. _____

8. _____

9. _____

10. _____

## Get noticed

To get your messages across, you will need to get noticed. It doesn't have to be sensational, but it does have to grab the attention of the media in an age when everybody wants to be famous.

## Thought leadership

A way you can effectively position yourself, both in terms of engaging the media and putting across your key messages, is to become a 'Thought Leader'. This means being recognized for innovative ideas and insights.

Becoming known as a 'Thought Leader' will mean you will be approached by journalists for expert comment, and your ideas will be discussed in business circles. You can use such opportunities to promote your key messages; this will help you shape the context that your business operates within.

## Move on the news agenda

In every interaction with the media, you should attempt to move on the news agenda. This enables you to work with the natural dynamics of the media, providing journalists with fresh insights that in turn create new stories.

## HINT BOX

Simon Howson-Green is a London-based PR professional and Managing Director of To The Point PR Agency. Here, he provides *Buy Me!* with his practical no-nonsense 'Dos and Don'ts' for making contact with the media:

### *The Dos*

- *Do make sure you know what the story is before you contact a journalist – they are only interested in you if you have a story.*

- *Do make sure you are speaking to the right person – if you contact a news desk these days, quite often the phone will be answered by an intern who has no power whatsoever apart from to stop you getting to the person you need to sell your story to. So be nice and clear, and work out who you need to speak to. Do, wherever possible, call and ask for a journalist by name – it will increase your chances of getting through no end.*

- *Do give the impression that the journalist already knows, or should know, who you are – and if they don't, they are at fault and not you. You can achieve this through being polite, not by sounding arrogant.*

- *Do make sure you focus on one thing: you have a story that the journalist would like to tell. No journalist – repeat – no journalist will ever put the phone down on you before they have heard what the story is, so make it a good story.*

- *Do make sure you know something of the work of the media organization or the journalist you are contacting. Don't try to tell a story to a journalist who is not interested in your subject.*

## HINT BOX

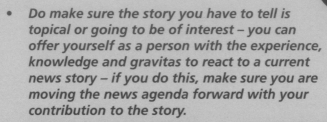

- *Do make sure the story you have to tell is topical or going to be of interest – you can offer yourself as a person with the experience, knowledge and gravitas to react to a current news story – if you do this, make sure you are moving the news agenda forward with your contribution to the story.*

- *Do be smart about the way you present yourself to the journalist. If you have a website or other information which may be useful, make sure you highlight this – chances are that if you have got the journalist's attention, they will Google you while you are talking to them.*

- *Do make sure you know more about the story than the journalist – in other words, make the journalist feel you are a good source ... so make sure you are.*

- *Do make sure if the journalist is interested in your story that they have all your contact details and you get theirs.*

- *Do make sure you present yourself as someone who is worth putting in the journalist's contact book – they all have them and they use them.*

- *Do ALWAYS offer to back up your call with an email laying out the facts of the story. This will help the journalist sell your story to the news editors.*

## The Don'ts

- *Don't offer to buy dinner or lunch for the journalist when you first make contact – do not promote anything but the story. You need to get*

## HINT BOX

the journalist to agree to meet you by suggesting it him- or herself.

- Don't confuse the journalist with too much information – stick to the story.
- Don't make your story about compromising someone else; leave that to politicians, game show hosts and Max Clifford – they are experts at it.
- Don't think a phone call is enough. Journalists have memories of elephants when it comes to stories and memories of goldfish when it comes to potential stories – consolidate your call.
- Don't let the contact slip. Decide which five journalists are most useful to you and cultivate a relationship with them – something along the lines of coffee or a catch-up phone call once a month, or a beer when you are next in town.
- Don't embellish your story or be economical with the truth – you will get caught out and your credibility will be blown.
- Don't be shy. Speaking to a journalist is spookily unnerving but remember that at this stage they need you because they need to tell stories – you hold all the cards.
- Don't be coy about exclusivity. If the story you are telling is a good one, offer it exclusively.
- Don't sell the story, sell yourself. Here is the big difference. You are attempting to get yourself into the media in order to sell yourself. This is not about flogging a story. You are not planning to make a living selling stories to the media.

# Section 2: New media

## The importance of new media

In the modern business world, the worldwide growth of the Internet means that new forms of media are now increasingly important. Our own business MBA & Company has been totally transformed by the Internet. We represent a global community of MBA graduates from the world's top twenty-five business schools. We used to personally visit companies, find out their consultancy needs, individually match them to MBA graduates who would then complete projects we would oversee. Now the entire process is online – we have projects around the world in countries such as Australia, France, the US, Brazil to South Africa, the UK, Spain and Kazakhstan. Our business model has been revolutionized by the Internet and the business has been able to dramatically increase in scale.

## Social media

Social media can enable you to achieve your own revolution in selling yourself. You can achieve great results at work, and have all the skills and qualities required, but unless you can develop a successful strategy to promote your selling proposition to the public, you will not fully benefit from it. In the same way the most talented people could stay neglected without mass media serving their interest, the best professionals and potential businesses would not succeed without a social media strategy.

A recent Jobvite Survey showed that 95 per cent of companies use Linkedin, 50 per cent use Facebook and 42 per cent use Twitter for recruitment. There are 90 million users in Linkedin, around 30 million users in Viadeo and 10 million users in XING. All of these users are professionals offering the complete range of vocational qualities and experiences.

How can you ensure your profile will be not only visible but also appealing?

## Focus on your target

The target you developed as part of Step 1 is key to your Internet profile. Your profile should reflect what you want to achieve in your life.

Use social media to search and study the profiles of other people who have already achieved the position you want or already work for the company you are targeting. Examine the qualities and skills required.

One of the most useful aspects of social media is communication. Social media platforms enable you to talk to people, share experiences and canvass for advice. Use the information you gain from other people to tailor your profile so that it is attractive to the public, promotes your candidacy or business, and attracts potential customers.

## Unique Selling Points (USPs)

To enhance your profile further, add the Unique Selling Points you also developed in 'Step 1: Self-belief and Confidence'. Adapt these points for social media based on the feedback you have received from communicating with other people.

## Position yourself

What are the most important messages to communicate on social media in order to create an outstanding business reputation?

Briefly explain your current position, what you are doing at the moment, and where you stand right now. Also, provide your past experience which is needed for others to understand and evaluate your career path. By underlining it, you are allowing the reader to understand the full range of the professional experiences you hold.

## Network

A glance at any social network website such as Linkedin shows the size of the network that supports the profiles. Having a broad network indicates you are socially active, popular, and therefore potentially useful or important.

In order to build your network, you can participate in different interest groups, forums, blogs. This can not only extend your social network but also create additional opportunities for your career growth, as your profile is becoming available to more potential recruiters or business partners.

## Get your message right

Your profile on a social network represents the personal brand you are creating, which can either help or hinder you. The sentences you add as a summary to your profile should contain powerful messages to reach your target. There are several ways to structure your summary in order to emphasize:

- Industries you are experienced in

- Your key activities

- Your professional qualities.

For instance, if you have a broad scope of industries that you have been involved in during your career, it is worth listing them:

'Over five years' professional experience with consulting projects in hospitality, pharmaceutical, automobile, media, FMCG.'

While writing about your activities, it is crucial not to underestimate the power of active verbs since they can considerably change the readers' impression of you.

Look at the table below and pick the verbs that mostly correspond to your profile:

*Accomplished   Achieved   Actively involved*

*Directly participated   Elaborated   Planned   Performed*

*Studied   Managed   Excelled   Formulated   Designed*

*Produced   Supervised   Diversified   Formed   Executed*

*Constructed   Initiated   Recruited   Trained   Negotiated*

*Mastered   Developed   Presented*

Write down the verbs which describe your activities and which appeal to you the most. Make sure these correspond to the requirement of the position you are targeting. Rank them according to the position you are targeting – which verbs in the list match with the qualities needed for the position you want? At the end, you should end up with the list that meets the requirements of your targeted job.

Now relate each of your achievements to the qualities needed for it. For example:

1.  Presented the results of market analysis to the Steering Committee, which required strong presentational skills.

2.  I actively participated in strategy development due to my strength in problem solving and flexibility in approach.

3.  _____

    _____

4.  _____

    _____

5.  _____

    _____

While describing your professional qualities, you should create your unique selling proposition. Pose this question to yourself: what are the qualities you would be searching for in you, if you were a potential recruiter? Think of your main achievements and strengths and use these to create your unique selling proposition. Take your recent position and look at your main achievements; now write down what personal qualities enabled you to achieve these. For example:

> Considered as a fast learner, out-of-box thinker, flexible approach, strong interpersonal skills, ability to adapt to a new environment, team player, multilingual approach, negotiation skills, fast problem solver, results-driven and highly qualified professional, demonstrating extensive experience, strength in data analysis, ability to adapt to a new environment.

Now you can see what your strongest qualities are, the ones which have allowed you to accomplish your main achievements in your life so far.

## Execute the new media strategy

Your aims in using social media should be clearly understood. Moreover, you should be consistent and honest – both with your friends on Facebook and with your colleagues on Linkedin. Due to the availability of information, inconsistency can substantially damage your online reputation. A recent survey found that 75 per cent of recruiters are screening the potential candidate's background on Linkedin and 48 per cent on Facebook, and it's been revealed that 35 per cent of employers refuse to hire the applicant after such a check. Therefore, the value of the information provided increases significantly while you communicate to the public via social media.

## Analyse, adapt and improve

It is crucial to be open to feedback and to adapt fast. If you are not reaching your goals, there are always opportunities to analyse the reasons why that is and to adjust your strategy. Here again the social network can be a useful tool. Share the information and feedback on forums and blogs, studying the profiles of those who do succeed. This will help you to understand what is missing from your overall social media strategy in promoting your profile.

## Be responsible about what you share

As already mentioned, it has become standard practice at many firms to search the social media profile of potential employees, suppliers and business partners. Therefore, you should not add details about personal social activities to your professional profile. For example, how much someone enjoys clubbing and partying may be part of their private Facebook profile but should not be added to a Linkedin profile. In the long term, the transparency of information and the need to continuously network to stay employed will probably mean that it is difficult to keep two distinct identities, i.e. personal and professional. Rather, you should be aware that everything you say stays on the record.

## HINT BOX

### Become Viral

*The most powerful way of becoming well known and reaching as many people as possible in the digital age is through a 'Viral Web Strategy'. This means that your website has independent systems which spread it from person to person like a virus. Max Levchin who founded PayPal (which he sold after four years for $1.5 billion to eBay) explained how a viral strategy was at the heart of his business:*

> *'We built the system to be viral from day one. The idea was: I can send you the money, even if you aren't a member. If I send you $10, you get an email saying, "You have $10 waiting for you. Sign up, and you can take it." That's the most powerful viral driver there is. Free money available to you.*
>
> *'For eBay buyers and sellers, it became this crazy loop where buyers would be like, "I want to pay you with PayPal," and sellers would be like, "I don't accept PayPal." And buyers would say, "That's OK. I'll just send you $10, and you can sign up." So the seller would get infected, and the seller would say, "Oh, this is really simple, so I only accept PayPal." '*

**Max Levchin, quoted in *Founders at Work* (2008)**

A self-perpetuating viral strategy is a key differentiator for the truly successful Internet companies.

# Case study: Mark Zuckerberg and the Facebook revolution

The story of Mark Zuckerberg, founder of Facebook, shows the incredible impact that you can have if you manage the media successfully in the information and digital age.

Zuckerberg joined Harvard University in September 2002 to study computer science. He had a talent for programming and as a teenager he had already developed software that 'learned' what music you liked. Microsoft reputedly offered the young Zuckerberg $1 million for the rights to the software.

## 'White board' thinking

At Harvard, Zuckerberg had brought with him a white ideas board that was so large it could only fit on the wall outside his dorm room. Passers-by would notice him staring at the white board for hours on end and writing new ideas for computer programs on it. His life was centred on computers, and he was always either searching the Internet or writing computer coding.

He used his talents to create a program called 'Facemash' that ranked female students against each other based on their looks. It became so popular that it generated approximately 20,000 hits in one night, crashing Harvard's Internet system. It was becoming clear that Zuckerberg had developed a unique understanding of what people looked for on the Internet.

## The Facebook

Harvard University had a thriving entrepreneurial culture, and it was not uncommon for students to be setting up businesses from their dorm rooms. So people were not too surprised to hear that Zuckerberg created a social network called 'The Facebook'. Shortly before, he had been using a social network called 'Friendster', which had imploded through its own popularity. Friendster developed technical problems as its servers struggled to handle the huge demand. At the time, there was another rapidly growing social network: Myspace.com. On this site people tended to indulge their creative sides, with fake names, elaborately decorated pages and new friendships with people they hadn't met before. The Facebook, however, required your real identity as verified by a Harvard email address.

The Facebook facilitated one central action that drove its growth faster than any other form of media in history: 'The only thing you could do immediately was invite more friends. It was that pureness which drove it'. (*The Facebook Effect*, 2010).

With a powerful viral growth strategy, The Facebook spread through each university it launched at, captivating over 50 per cent of students in a few days. It also harnessed a strategy to keep people coming back to the site. Notifications would alert people to new comments, friend requests and photographs, meaning that people were constantly returning to the site. The Facebook was in fact engaging web users in a more powerful way than any other website had done before, with most users returning to the site daily for long periods of time.

Sean Parker, a founder of the dot-com businesses Napster and Plaxo, joined The Facebook's team. He brought to the company an understanding of the venture capitalist community that funded technology start-ups in the US. Parker's VC pitch and the social network's astonishing user statistics drew round after round of multimillion dollar investment for the newly named 'Facebook'.

## Truly new media

While refusing many traditional online advertising opportunities, Zuckerberg learned how to make money from his invention. Facebook provided advertisers for the first time with an Internet site that validated identity and provided extensive information on each individual. The result is the ability to complete highly successful targeted advertising campaigns.

Another compelling commercial aspect of Facebook is its role as a 'platform'. Bill Gates created a platform when he provided the software for PC – which other people depend on to make products for the Internet – helping to make him one of the wealthiest men in the world. Facebook has also become a platform, allowing applications to use its site for free in order to generate business. The Facebook platform turns the social connections of Facebook users into an economy, on top of which businesses can grow.

The Facebook team have continued to push the boundaries between what people are willing to share on the Internet. As the social barriers came down, Facebook spread around the world. At the time of writing, Facebook has more than 500 million users, many of whom spend hours on the site each day, which makes it the most widely used and compelling media platform in history.

The financial value of this kind of mass appeal was clear in 2011 when Goldman Sachs sold on shares of Facebook to Digital Sky Technologies, valuing the company at $50 billion. Mark Zuckerberg is now the youngest billionaire in the world.

## ✓ What you have learned about managing the media

In this chapter, you have learned how to manage traditional and new media. This has included positioning yourself as a 'Thought Leader' and handling interviews with journalists. You have also seen how to create your unique selling proposition out of your professional profile, as well as how to emphasize your qualities, achievements, and the importance of choosing the right channels and tools to promote it. You have also learned about the power of managing the media in the digital age, offering you the opportunity to become well known on a scale never before possible.

# Step 10:
## Leadership

'Before you are a leader, success is
all about growing yourself.
When you become a leader, success is
all about growing others.'
**Jack Welch**

## Why is leadership important?

Leadership is one of the most powerful drivers of human behaviour. The ability to motivate other people towards your goals and your objectives can enable you to achieve almost anything.

In business, individually proving your worth will enable you to stay employable. However, it will not ensure that you are offered management responsibility or that you are able to grow your own business. In order to sell yourself well enough to reach the upper echelons of business, you will need to inspire others by being an effective leader.

# How this chapter will help you with leadership

Learn important facts on how to inspire others, including:

*Individual leadership:*

- *Create a leadership vision*
- *Lead by example*
- *Empower others*
- *Create a meritocracy*
- *Manage bad performance*
- *Be self-aware*
- *Value differences*

*Leading a team:*

- *Awakening*
- *Antagonizing*
- *Assimilating*
- *Accomplishing*

# Section 1: Individual leadership

## Create a leadership vision

As a leader your first question should be: 'Where will I lead people towards?' You need to develop a shared leadership vision that is:

- **Motivating** – Descriptive of a future scenario which all stakeholders will wish to belong and contribute to.

- **Realistic** – Perceived to be achievable. Few things are more demotivating than one objective that you know from the beginning cannot be reached. Perhaps the goal is very ambitious and challenging, but there must always be the belief that it has the potential to become a serious reality one day.

- **Flexible** – Able to deal with different developments and scenarios that may emerge.

- **Communicated** – Understood and communicated in a clear and simple manner.

- **Shared** – The benefits are not only for you but for the whole team. You must aim to fulfil others and not only yourself.

## Lead by example

Your team need to know they can rely on you to deliver 100 per cent, and this will encourage them to give their best too. To get other people deeply involved, there should be alignment between your behaviour and your vision. Good sports team captains are great examples of leading by example; they can embody the values and ambitions of the team within themselves and their performance. Several great historical leaders have actually sacrificed their lives for their vision. Among these is Mahatma Gandhi who expressed the importance of consistence between vision and action in his inspirational statement, 'You must be the change you wish to see in the world'.

## Empower others

People respond well to working situations in which they have influence over decision-making. Therefore, in order to get the most of the people you lead, it is necessary to share control and responsibilities. However good you are at a certain role or task, there will always be another way of achieving it even better. Good leadership is not prescribing a set of tasks and monitoring them but, rather, enabling people to flourish and perform to the best of their abilities. Achieving this type of engagement means giving people ownership over their own projects and responsibilities. Supportive guidance, not insistent instruction, is the hallmark of a good leader. This will create engaged employees motivated to work for you, and eager to achieve your and the organization's objectives. As Dwight Eisenhower said: 'Leadership is the art of getting someone else to do something you want done because he wants to do it'.

## Create a meritocracy

While it may be an unfavourable comparison, leading people has parallels with raising children or even family pets. Professionals who train dogs do so with positive encouragement. When the dog does something good, this is seized on and it is rewarded with praise, attention and treats. Human beings also respond to positive encouragement. When you notice a team member doing something right, then lavish praise on them and it will encourage them to do the same again. Rewarding good performance should form part of a broader meritocratic culture amongst your team or organization. People who perform well should receive encouragement, reward and promotion. This will ensure the best people you manage are motivated, put in the right positions and retained.

## Manage bad performance

When training, it is not beneficial to reprimand those who perform badly. Mistakes should be expected as there is a learning curve of trial and error.

For experienced team members who perform badly, it is also not useful to punish, humiliate or offer threats. It is good practice to conduct regular reviews with your team so that you can explore issues such as why they are not performing satisfactorily and how you can help them to perform better. This will ensure that you provide all the resources needed to improve their performance, and that you do not alienate them and lose their motivation.

## Be self-aware

As covered earlier in Step 5: Empathy, emotional intelligence is a key aspect that employers look out for in employees with leadership skills. Being self-aware and self-regulating is highly important in effective leadership. As a leader, your role is to have an impact on your team, but you need to be constantly self-aware to ensure that you are having the right impact. A useful tool is the 360-degree appraisal in which you receive feedback not just from your superiors but also from those you manage. This can enable you to fully understand the positive and negative impact you are having on those you lead.

## Value differences

The people you lead will probably have strengths and weaknesses in different areas, so do not expect the same performance in all tasks from everyone. Personality type indicators, such as the Myers-Briggs one, classify people on a spectrum of thinking versus feeling, and planning versus intuitive. This serves to highlight that some people are naturally inclined to be organized and enjoy planning, while others prefer to leave things open and be spontaneous. There is no wrong or right way, and different people will fit better into different roles based on their preferences.

In the modern globalized economy, it is also important to be aware of cultural differences. There is evidence that nationalities with distinct cultures have different attitudes. For example, in the 1960s and 1970s, Geert Hofstede carried out a survey on 116,000 IBM employees across forty countries. The study discovered differences in cultural attitudes on a range of areas:

- **Power distance** – The extent to which members of a society consent to power being distributed unequally in organizations, e.g. manager–subordinate relationships.

- **Uncertainty avoidance** – The extent to which a society manages the ambiguity of the future, and if people feel threatened by uncertainty.

- **Collectivism / Individualism** – The degree to which the society reinforces individual or collective achievement and interpersonal relationships.

- **Masculinism** – The division and application of masculine / feminine roles and values within the society, such as concern for others versus aggression.

Understanding such cultural differences does not mean racially profiling and stereotyping people, but instead appreciating and valuing other approaches.

## Charismatic Leadership

By demonstrating exceptional self-belief, charm and grace through leadership, some people can develop admiration and loyalty in others, known as 'charisma'. Julius Caesar used his charismatic leadership skills to develop one of the greatest hand-to-hand fighting forces ever known, and he changed the course of history by bringing about the end of the Roman Republic.

Julius Caesar is one of the most powerful and important figures in history. He was an orator, a historian, a statesman and a legislator, and an unstoppable army general. Believing his family lineage to descend from the goddess Venus and the royal Trojan prince Aeneas, Caesar showed incredible self-belief from his earliest years.

As a young man, while he was travelling to study public speaking, he was kidnapped by pirates who held him for ransom. Completely unintimidated, during the day he would take all exercises with his captors. In the evening he read poetry to them, spitting the words in their faces if they didn't listen. He told them they could ask for a much higher ransom for someone of his status, and also that he would one day return to execute them all. On release, he did indeed assume command of some troops, return and kill all his captors, showing mercy by slitting their throats so they could die quickly.

He returned to Rome and made a successful political career for himself by using his excellent oratory skills.He ran for the position of Princeps telling his mother that 'Caesar would return as Princeps or would not return at all'. He won office and his power and influence grew in Rome, as he entered into the first Triumvirate in Roman history. This meant he allied with the two most powerful figures in Rome, Pompei Magnus and Crassus. The combined power of the three and their followers in the Senate, meant they could control Rome.

Caesar used this influence to win appointment as Proconsul of Gaul, becoming head of one of the largest Roman regions.

Caesar had a unique charisma as a leader and to enforce his rule in Gaul he built arguably the greatest hand-to-hand fighting force in history. He achieved this using many of the leadership elements found in modern management. He led by example, and in training he would play 'find Caesar', with troops running after him on his horse for hours. On the battlefield, he placed himself among his soldiers, quickly riding to any weak spots to coach and support them. He also installed principles of meritocracy in his army. Soldiers knew that good performance would be rewarded both financially and through promotion. Caesar would provide cash rewards and publicly name excellent soldiers.

As Caesar conquered Gaul he wrote his own memoirs, creating his own version of history which is still influential today. He was a Latin scholar and, remarkably, while campaigning he also found time to complete studies, which made improvements to Latin grammar. His ambition even led him to stage a short invasion of a country that was seen as highly exotic and strange in the Roman world, Great Britain.

Eventually, Caesar grew so powerful that he came into conflict with the Roman Republic itself. A civil war ensued and ended at Pharsallus, when Caesar's military strategy and the steadfast loyalty and discipline of his troops defeated the opposing Roman general Pompei Magnus. The result was effectively the end of the Roman Republic, and the beginning of the age of the Caesars, changing the entire course of history. Caesar was assasinated at the age of fifty-five, but through a unique charismatic leadership developed a 'prestige' which has lived on for two millennia.

## HINT BOX

### Charismatic Leadership

*Tips to improve your charisma are:*
- *Demonstrate absolute belief in your vision*
- *Use body language to support your verbal communication*
- *Make sacrifices for the values and ambitions of your vision*
- *Make every individual feel highly valued*
- *Make your group feel secure and superior to others*

# Section 2: Leading a team

As a leader, one of your most important roles is to lead and increase the performance of your team. Researchers such as Bruce Tuckman and Tannenbaum and Schmidt have shown that the dynamics of teams go through comparable phases. These phases have been compiled into models in Ken Blanchard's 'Situational Leadership' and Bruce Tuckman's 'Form, Storm, Norm, Perform'. The common themes of these phases can be summed up in awakening, antagonizing, assimilating, accomplishing:

## Awakening

In the first phase of a team, individuals get to know one another. This period is characterized by:

- Desire for acceptance

- Serious issues avoided

- Impressions being made

- Individuals working quite independently.

As the leader of the group, there is a high dependence on you for guidance and direction. You must be prepared to answer a lot of questions and provide:

- A shared understanding of the team's purpose

- Clear expectations about the roles and responsibilities of team members

- Set values and acceptable behaviours for working together.

## Antagonizing

After a team has formed, it goes through a challenging time of 'antagonization', characterized by the team:

- Addressing issues and beginning to solve problems
- Opening up and challenging each other's ideas and points of view
- Splitting into factions
- Competing for power and attention
- Developing negative feelings such as confusion and low trust.

As the leader, in this difficult phase you are needed to clarify the big picture and overall objectives. You are also required to restate the values, goals and objectives of the teams. Your communication skills are also important here, in providing constructive feedback and facilitating open and honest discussion.

## Assimilating

During this period, the team begins to positively assimilate with each other, characterized by the team:

- Developing shared goals
- Developing trust and respect
- Giving up some of their own ideas and adopting those of others.

As the leader, you are required to reinforce the positive integration of the team. You should encourage the building of trust, the sharing of perspectives and also recognize the successes of the team.

## Accomplishing

In the final phase, the team begins 'accomplishing' and this phase is characterized by:

- Clear understanding of objectives and mutual plans
- Shared responsibility and working together for the success of the team's goals
- Open and trusting communication
- Respect and appreciation for each other
- Positive feelings such as confidence and high morale.

Now, there is a high respect for the leader whose role becomes one of facilitation and enablement. It is important to recognize the team's achievements and provide new challenges, opportunities for growth and learning.

Overall, leading a team means recognizing that it is not enough to simply get the tasks done well; it is also important to develop and maintain the group's cohesion, harmony and unity. The role of the leader is to move the team through the different stages of development. This also means that if the team regresses and goes back to an earlier stage, it is necessary to apply the leadership suitable for that circumstance. Ultimately, a good leader is one who achieves a high-performing team that has little need for their management.

# Case study:
# Jack Welch's transformational
# leadership

One of the greatest of all business leaders is Jack Welch, who has been called 'CEO of the century'. Welch's leadership has seen him become an almost mythological figure in the US and international business community.

Jack Welch became the youngest CEO of General Electric (GE) in 1981, when he was only forty-four years old. General Electric was an enormous company turning over billions of dollars. However, it was also involved in many sectors where it was not particularly successful. There were many layers of management and the company was in need of dramatic reform.

## Against bureaucracy

One of the first revolutions launched after Welch became CEO of GE was his battle against bureaucracy – he cut almost all nine levels of hierarchy found at the time of his inauguration as Chief Executive. You can imagine how difficult such a change may have been for a company as big as GE but this turned out to be one of Welch's most important acts.

Welch established direct contact with thousands of his employees every year through unexpected company visits. This allowed him to exert strong leadership by example on the entire company, and gave him the chance to act as facilitator for the transfer of ideas between the various divisions of GE. He compared his company to a small corner grocer's shop because he liked communications within the organization to be simple with everyone involved.

Thanks to Welch, we now have the concept of feedback models so that everyone can effectively have their say. The effectiveness of this organizational strategy is now recognized by many analysts who marvel at the flexibility and dynamism of a company this size (especially since GE was able to maintain double-digit growth rates almost continuously throughout Welch's time in office).

## People

For Welch the core competency was people. During his years at GE, he always devoted more than 50 per cent of his time to people activities (asking managers to do the same with their staff). Welch invested a great amount in General Electric's training facility, Crotonville, and this became the centre of cultural change. As CEO, Welch actually directly participated in the evaluation of more than 3,000 managers and monitored closely the development of the top 500 managers of the company. According to Welch, there are four characteristics of a high-potential manager and these can be easily summed up with '4E' (as befits any good theory of management):

- **Energy:** the ability to address every problem and situation with passion and proactivity.

- **Energized:** the ability to motivate and energize those around us.

- **Edge:** the ability to make decisions without doubts and questions.

- **Execution:** the ability to implement strategies and bring results.

Those who possess these characteristics are usually the top 20 per cent of managers and those on whom the company should always focus their efforts. This is achieved by differentiated pay attention in line with the performance of the best performers. Welch put into practice this concept by creating a pay system that offered bonuses and stock options of up to 70 per cent of the basic salary of managers.

## No. 1 and No. 2

Welch installed a business philosophy and strategy that states that GE should be No. 1 or No. 2 in all the business it owns, and sell or close those in which it isn't. This strategy has become accepted practice at diversified multinational companies, but it was originally developed and brought to success by Jack Welch's great capacity for strategic vision.

In fact, in a period when the majority of business schools taught the virtues of concentration on a limited number of businesses to leverage the core competencies, or all the knowledge and synergies resulting from specialists in the field, Welch preached and practised the advantages of differentiation, making over 600 acquisitions in various sectors. The main factor for deciding on the acquisition/disposal was likely to be based on whether the company was the leader (or co-leader) in its market. In all cases where this was not the case, there were three alternatives: to bring the company to GE standard, sell it or close it.

Jack Welch's transformational leadership was so successful that during his twenty-year tenure (Welch reached retirement age in 2001) he created as much value as any other manager in history, bringing the market capitalization of GE from 'only' $12 billion to over $360 billion (No. 1 in the world) at the time of his retirement.

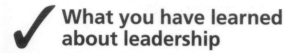

## What you have learned about leadership

In this chapter, you have learned how to lead individuals effectively and create high-performing teams. The emphasis has been on inspiring others with responsibility and ownership, rather than controlling them with discipline. This will enable you to create engaged teams who want to work for you, are able to fulfil themselves professionally and aspire to work to the best of their abilities. We saw in the case of Jack Welch the power of a people-centred approach in achieving business results. The end result of such a leadership strategy will be achievement of your shared ambitions.

# Final Thoughts

## The future of selling yourself

This book has presented ten steps to sell yourself based on the latest business school and management theory, as well as on real-life experience and examples. Having self-belief, being prepared, over-delivering, having empathy, going the extra mile, managing the media (whether it be the printing press or the social network) and inspiring others are timeless steps to success in any age.

However, if fundamental approaches to selling yourself can be maintained, the context in which you do it does change dramatically. These shifts often follow what Malcolm Gladwell called 'tipping points', or what Nassim Nicholas Taleb described as 'black swans'. These unexpected, largely unpredictable events create a sea change in the economic landscape. The best example of this in recent history is the rise of the Internet.

### Changing times

The Internet has changed the world, and it has fundamentally changed business. Certain industries such as publishing have been at the forefront of these changes and have borne the brunt of the impact on the bottom line. What better example of 'disintermediation', or losing an intermediary role, than the replacement in market share of the newspaper, the magazine and the book by the news website, the iPhone app and the eReader. The response from publishers has been to incorporate the digital into the way they engage with consumers, and in years to come they may be better placed than other sectors for having done so.

Almost every aspect of our lives is being incorporated into the Internet. For example, Google managed to translate the way that books order the relevance of information into an effective way of searching the Internet. Facebook translated young people's natural interest in their friends into an online social network. Linkedin reinterpreted the professional networks that develop in economies into an online portal. Groupon has capitalized on the consumer's natural desire for a bargain, with an online discount coupon community. Therefore, evaluating what aspects of your life or business can be successfully moved online is a very good way of developing the businesses of tomorrow.

The Internet has caused the largest recent paradigm shift in business but it will not be the last. The next major change may be the rise of India and China, and the shift of economic power to the East. If this is the case, the question becomes, 'How do I develop my business in China over the next fifteen years?' Whatever the new context, swimming with and not against the current by preplanning for the next sea change is another useful way of developing future high-growth businesses.

In the first half of the twentieth century, the focus for much of the aspiring middle class was on qualifying for a steady profession, such as a doctor or lawyer. Meanwhile, the working class looked for 'a job for life' at a company or in the public sector. Both looked to rely on stable jobs that would support them throughout their careers. In the twenty-first century, this stability no longer exists, and it is likely that you will have many jobs, at many companies, interacting with businesses all over the world. You will need to develop new skills and follow new trends in an economy that constantly changes. Therefore, the right approach for business people at the beginning of the twenty-first century is to continually learn, adapt and change in the context of changing business paradigms.

To achieve the right versatility in this modern environment, you will need to constantly engage with companies, listen to your peers, understand their businesses, follow the news, and study the successes of other companies. In this regard, the skills you have developed in this book will provide an invaluable toolkit enabling you to successfully interact in the economy. Appreciating the value of constant engagement, we would like to learn from you and encourage your feedback, your thoughts, your stories and your interaction with each other. So, we invite you to contact us:

Adam Riccoboni
Adam@mbaanco.com

Daniel Callaghan
Daniel@mbaandco.com

As Alumni, or the graduates of *Buy Me!*, we expect a lot from you and look forward to seeing you at the top.

# Bibliography

Bar-On, R. 'Emotional and social intelligence: Insights from the Emotional Quotient Inventory (EQ-i)', in R. Bar-On & J.D.A. Parker (Eds.), *Handbook of Emotional Intelligence* pp. 363-88, Jossey-Bass, 2000

Batson, C. D., Sager K., Garst E., Kang M., Rubchinsky K., Dawson K. 'Is empathy induced helping due to self–other merging?' *Journal of Personality and Social Psychology* Vol 73 (3), pp. 495–509, 1997

Blair, Tony, *A Journey: My Political Life*, Hutchinson, 2010

Blanchard, Kenneth and Johnson, Spencer, *The One Minute Manager*, William Morrow, 1982

Bossidy, Larry and Charan, Ram, *Execution: The Discipline of Getting Things Done*, Crown, 2002

Bossidy, Larry and Charan, Ram, *Confronting Reality: Doing What Matters to Get Things Right*, Crown, 2004

Branson, Sir Richard, *Losing My Virginity*, Crown Business, 1999

Bruna Martinuzzi, *The Leader as a Mensch: Become the Kind of Person Others Want to Follow*, Six Seconds, 2009

Charan, Ram, *What the CEO Wants You to Know: How Your Company Really Works*, Crown, 2001

Collins, Jim, *Good to Great: Why Some Companies Make the Leap ... And Others Don't*, HarperBusiness, 2001

Corcoran, K. J. 'An exploratory investigation into self–other differentiation: Empirical evidence for a monistic perspective of empathy.' *Psychotherapy: Theory, Research and Practice* Vol 19 (1) pp. 63–8, 1982

Dennis, Felix, *How to Get Rich*, Portfolio, 2009

Duan, C., & Hill, C. E., 'The current state of empathy research.' *Journal of Counselling Psychology* Vol 43 (3) pp. 261–74, 1996

Keith Eades, *The New Solution Selling*, McGraw-Hill, 2003

Eisenberg, N., Fabes, R. A., Murphy, B., Karbon, M., Maszk, P., Smith, M., O'Boyle, C., Suh, K., 'The relations of emotionality and regulation to dispositional and situation empathy-related responding' *Journal of Personality and Social Psychology* Vol 66 (4) pp.776-97, 1994

Gerdes, K. E., Segal E. A., 'The importance of empathy for social work practice: Integrating new science', *Social Work*, in press, 2010

Gladwell, Malcolm, *The Tipping Point: How Little Things Make a Big Difference*, Abacus, 2002

Goldsworthy, Adrian, *Caesar: The Life of a Colossus*, Yale University Press, 2008

Goleman, Daniel, *Emotional Intelligence: Why It Can Matter More Than IQ*, Bloomsbury, 1995

Goleman, Daniel, *Working With Emotional Intelligence*, Bloomsbury, 1999

Goleman, Daniel, *Social Intelligence: The New Science of Human Relationships*, Arrow, 2007

Graham, Benjamin, *The Intelligent Investor*, HarperCollins, 2003

Gross, J. J., 'The emerging field of emotion regulation: *An integrative review*', *Review of General Psychology* Vol 2 (3) pp.271–99, 1998

Hartman, Amir, *Ruthless Execution: What Business Leaders Do When Their Companies Hit the Wall*, FT Press, 2003

Hutchins, P., The Body Shop International PLC: Ruby campaign, *Encyclopedia of Major Marketing Campaigns*, Vol 2, pp. 191–94, 2007

Iannarino, S.A., '5 Ways to Improve Your Empathy and EQ in Sales', http://thesalesblog.com/2010/02/5-ways-to-improve-your-empathy-and-eq-in-sales/, Accessed on 1 February, 2011

Ickes, W., Stinson, L., Bissonnette, V., Garcia, S. 'Naturalistic social cognition: Empathic accuracy in mixed-sex dyads.' *Journal of Personality and Social Psychology*, Vol 59 (4) pp. 730-42 1990

Jolliffe, D., Farrington, D. P., 'Development and validation of the Basic Empathy Scale.' *Journal of Adolescence*, Vol 29, pp. 589-611, 2006

Jones, Peter, *Tycoon: How to Turn Dreams Into Millions*, Hodder & Stoughton, 2007

Kirkpatrick, David, *The Facebook Effect*, Simon & Schuster, 2011

Lawrence, E. J., Shaw, P., Baker, D., Baron-Cohen, S., David, A. S. 'Measuring empathy: Reliability and validity of the empathy quotient.' *Psychological Medicine*, Vol 34 pp. 911-24, 2004

Livingstone, Jessica, *Founders At Work: Stories of Startups' Early Days*, Apress, 2008

Polychroniou, P.V., 'Relationship between emotional intelligence and transformational leadership of supervisors: the impact on team effectiveness', *Team Performance Management* Vol. 15 (7/8), pp. 343–56, 2008

Rackham, Neil, *SPIN-selling*, McGraw-Hill, 1988

Rasiel, Ethan, *The McKinsey Mind: Understanding and Implementing the Problem-Solving Tools and Management Techniques of the World's Top Strategic Consulting Firm*, McGraw-Hill, 2001

Roddick, A, DISPATCH: Ruby, the Anti-Barbie, http://www.anitaroddick.com/readmore.php?sid+13, Accessed on 4 February, 2011

Ryan Jr, Bernard, *Jeff Bezos*, Ferguson Publishing Company, 2005

Schroeder, Alice, *The Snowball: Warren Buffet and the Business of Life*, Bloomsbury, 2009

Singh, K., 'Emotional Intelligence & Workplace Effectiveness' *IJIR*, Vol. 44 (2), 2008

Spreng R. N., McKinnon M. C., Mar R. A., Levine B. 'The Toronto empathy questionnaire: Scale development and initial validation of a factor-analytic solution to multiple empathy measures.' *Journal of Personality Assessment* Vol 91 (1) pp. 62–71, 2009

Taleb, Nassem Nicholas, *The Black Swan: The Impact of the Highly Improbable*, Penguin 2008

Trump, Donald, with Tony Scwhartz, *Trump: The Art of the Deal*, Ballantine Books, 2004

Welch, Jack, *Jack: Straight from the Gut*, Headline, 2003

Wispe, L., 'The distinction between sympathy and empathy: To call forth a concept a word is needed.' *Journal of Personality and Social Psychology* Vol 50 pp. 314–21, 1986

Yeung, Dr Rob, *Confidence: The Art of Getting Whatever You Want*, Prentice Hall Life, 2008

# Index